THE

REACH OUT

APPROACH

THE
REACH
OUT
APPROACH

A Communication Process for

INITIATING, DEVELOPING *&* LEVERAGING

Mutually Rewarding Relationships

STEVE GAVATORTA

Advantage®

Published by Advantage, Charleston, South Carolina.
Member of Advantage Media Group.

ADVANTAGE is a registered trademark and the Advantage colophon is a trademark of Advantage Media Group, Inc.

Printed in the United States of America.

ISBN: 978-1-59932-098-4
LCCN: 2008943366

This publication is designed to provide accurate and authoritative information in regard to the subject matter covered. It is sold with the understanding that the publisher is not engaged in rendering legal, accounting, or other professional services. If legal advice or other expert assistance is required, the services of a competent professional person should be sought.

Most Advantage Media Group titles are available at special quantity discounts for bulk purchases for sales promotions, premiums, fundraising, and educational use. Special versions or book excerpts can also be created to fit specific needs.

For more information, please write: Special Markets, Advantage Media Group, P.O. Box 272, Charleston, SC 29402 or call 1.866.775.1696.

Visit us online at **advantagefamily**.com

I dedicate this book to my parents, Steve and Donna Gavatorta for their love and constant support

ACKNOWLEDGMENTS

"He was not born a king of men...but a child of the common people, who made himself a great persuader, therefore a leader by dint of firm resolve, patient effort and dogged perseverance...He was open to all impressions and influences and gladly profited by the teachings of events and circumstances no matter how adverse or unwelcome. There was probably no year in my life when he was not a wiser, cooler and better man than he had been the year preceding."

- Horace Greeley on Abraham Lincoln -

This quote by Horace Greeley on Abraham Lincoln is one of my favorite quotes of all time. I find it highly motivational and a good standard to strive for in my life.

That said, I wanted to acknowledge all the people in my life who have similarly influenced and motivated me to live a life of constant improvement. People who not only motivated me, but also were patient and knew how to communicate with me in a way that allowed me to learn and grow. Who communicated with me in ways I could understand and which resonated with me. Who communicated with me to enable me to be the best person I could become in my life. For those people who push me to be the best I can be.

First and foremost, I would like to acknowledge my friend and mentor Santo Laquatra, whose guidance and wisdom I've been receiving for nearly twenty-eight years. My friend is never too busy or too tired to take the time to help not only me, but others as well. Truly selfless, he is a role model I seek to aspire to in my life.

My first personal coach, friend, mentor and oftentimes business partner, Meryl Moritz, whose sage advice provided me with the courage and guidance to get my business off the ground.

To my past corporate managers who had great confidence in me and taught me business fundamentals that helped me grow professionally. A special thanks to Santo, Tim Solt, Brian Siedlecki, Scott Jones, Gene Page, Jim Wade, Jim Shanahan, Rosemary Masse and Michael Roth.

To my sports coaches who had great confidence in me and taught me "character based" fundamentals that helped me grow personally. A special thanks to Mike Danna, John Barish, Homer Marshall, Joe Harvey, Pete Comis, Petro Maropis, John Spak, Terry Havelka, Rich Conley and Dan Slovick.

To great historical leaders who, through reading about them, inspire me every day – most notably Winston Churchill, but also Ronald Reagan, King David, Dick Winters, Helen Keller, Douglas MacArthur, Dwight Eisenhower, George Marshall and Abraham Lincoln to name a few.

To great motivators who, through reading their books, inspire me every day – most notably Stephen Covey, Wayne Dyer, Anthony Robbins, James Allen, Napoleon Hill and Jim Cathcart to name a few.

Sophfronia Scott, my editor, for giving the structure and roadmap to write this book and get it published. And Sam Horn for her great insights, witty ideas and support.

And last but not least my childhood friend Mark Marshall for his support and honest opinions.

Contents

LADIES AND GENTLEMEN, THIS IS A HUMAN BEING

The event was the National Speakers Association (NSA) Convention several years back and I was there to consider becoming a member and thinking about building my career as a public speaker. At the time, I'd coached and trained thousands of people for well over twenty years and had done a good deal of public speaking but I wanted to take that part of my business to a much higher level. So the NSA convention seemed like the logical place to start. Most of these conventions I'd attended have been helpful but I was never able to sustain long, meaningful relationships from them. I'd heard that the NSA was a superior organization with hundreds of wonderful people so I figured I would check it out for myself. At first though, it seemed like just another one of those same cliquish conventions.

After observing the initial keynote speaker, who was fantastic, I attended a dinner and sat at a table of strangers. As a first timer, not knowing anyone at the table, I found it hard to generate much conversation. Now I am not by nature a shy person, however several of the folks at the table already knew each other and others seemed focused on speaking about themselves so I spent most of the time listening versus truly meeting anyone. As I turned in for the evening I chalked it up to a single incident and thought the next day would be better.

Well, initially it was not. The first event I attended the next day consisted of a breakout session with about eight people at a table listening to an expert on a given topic. Some of the folks I sat with ranged from the mildly bizarre, a "fire walking" speaker, to the really bizarre, someone who spoke about "the art of witchcraft." And again, these were folks who seemingly wanted to talk about themselves versus learn new ideas, have a two-way dialogue and build relationships…not exactly what I was looking for at this event nor in my speaking career. I was beginning to think that the event was not going to be a productive venue for me.

That afternoon the keynote speaker was, again, excellent but I still had not felt the camaraderie I was looking for in such an event. Then, later that evening something happened that not only changed my viewpoint of the organization and influenced my decision to aggressively add speaking as an integral part of my core business, *but most importantly, it greatly strengthened my beliefs on the ability to and power of truly reaching out and connecting with people.*

Later that evening a friend and I met for a drink at the bar. Another fellow speaker soon joined us. We engaged in productive discussion and after an hour we noticed one of the most successful and popular speakers at the convention approaching us. His name is Tim Gard, and he is a much sought after speaker whose niche is comedy.

Tim joined our conversation and I found him very friendly, engaging and insightful. In fact, I was learning a great deal from him. I thoroughly enjoyed speaking with him. As time progressed however, more and more people approached our area to meet and speak with him. So what started out as a nice intimate discussion turned into a mob scene.

In fact, so many people came over to our table that Tim literally had his back to me so I couldn't even hear what he was saying anymore.

It was at that moment, Tim did something so subtle yet so powerful that it had a lasting effect on me until this very day. As he was talking to the group and without even turning around or looking directly at me, he reached behind and lighted grabbed my shoulder. The point he was making was that he knew I was there and that he had his back to me and wanted me to realize that he knew it. That subtle non-verbal communication blew me away. That subtle act of kindness, acknowledgement and connection showed me what type of person Tim Gard was, and what type of people were members of the NSA. It meant a great deal as so many of us forget that subtle acts to reach out and connect are so powerful. Later on Tim apologized for turning his back and I assured him that I recognized his effort and it meant a lot.

Soon thereafter, I was walking towards the convention hall to have dinner when I was approached by a speaker named Gary Rifkin to join him at the head table to dine with the president of NSA and other wonderful and successful speakers. I was approached because I had a "first time attendee" badge, and they wanted to *reach out* and welcome a first time attendee. The dinner could not have gone better and I was able to build some wonderful relationships with some great people. From that point on the remainder of the convention was outstanding. I met fabulous people and learned a lot. The ripple effect of the positive experiences continued throughout the convention. All of which had been initiated because of Tim Gard reaching out to me earlier that evening.

The next day, I ran into another friend and colleague, Sophfronia Scott, who recently started a new business of helping speakers get published.

I ran into her by accident. We talked for a while, and soon agreed to work together to help me publish my first book, in fact, the one you're reading right now. Could that one subtle gesture by Tim Gard to reach out and connect start such a positive ripple effect of running into her by accident as well? I think an affirmative YES!

The point of this story is that Tim Gard's subtle act of kindness, acknowledgment, non-verbal communication meant the world to me and truly changed my view of the organization and event. I felt that any organization that has people like Tim Gard as a member is an organization I want to become a member of. In addition, it turned out the organization was filled with Tim Gard-type folks as I found out at the president's table and throughout the remainder of the convention. From that point on the convention took on a new meaning for me. I met people, made new friends, and learned a ton and I am now a member of the NSA National and active member in the Central Florida Chapter and an accomplished public speaker. A great deal of that is due to one subtle yet powerful act of human interaction by Tim Gard to…*reach out.*

You see, when you make the effort to reach out you set in motion a series of events that can affect many lives, in the positive. It is like when you throw a stone in the water and consider the ripples it creates. The same is true in life. By reaching out, we all can have and create a positive ripple effect as well.

Lastly, I also realized that it doesn't take much to make differences in peoples lives. Subtle acts like Tim's can do the trick. It validated my belief that the ability to reach out, connect and make lasting impressions is still so powerful and the repercussions far reaching.

GENTLEMEN, THIS IS A FOOTBALL -
A LESSON FROM COACH VINCE LOMBARDI

Legendary Green Bay Packers' football coach Vince Lombardi was a man who believed that to be successful at football one had to have a firm understanding and mastery of the fundamentals of the game. In fact, he would start the first practice of every season by going right back to the basics. Holding it out in front of him, he would pronounce to a veteran group of professional athletes, "Gentlemen, THIS is a football." Now, his players were not kids in grade school, teens in high school or students in college. These were men playing professional football who had been playing for many years, in fact, almost their entire lives. They were professionals, the best of the best. Yet, Coach Lombardi knew that the success of his team depended on its mastery of the fundamentals. Hence, he always went back to the basics, re-introducing them to the football. In turn, he was making a very powerful point about the importance of fundamentals.

The purpose of this book is to empower you to master the art of effective communication and the first step is to re-introduce you to a key basic fundamental ingredient of this art, ***the human being***.

I believe that in the fast-paced, quick growth technological age, we are forgetting how to truly reach out, interact and connect with others and, hence, effectively communicate. We are getting caught up in so many external situations in our hectic lives – made more intense by the growth of the Internet, email and text messaging – that we are forgetting how to truly connect with people for effective communication.

So just as Coach Lombardi, continued to re-introduce the football as the most basic element for his team to master the sport of football, I am re-introducing you to the most basic element of effective communication...again, *the human being.*

A SUBTLE GESTURE THAT IGNITED
A SERIES OF EVENTS

In my story, Tim Gard remembered me, a human being, a person and made a subtle gesture to reach out, connect and, in turn, communicate to me, which spurred a list of positive repercussions. That is what I want to accomplish in this book – to get back to the basics of meaningful, effective communication.

When I say effective communication, I mean really making a long lasting impression through an emotional connection. When you touch an emotion, you reach someone in the deepest and most memorable ways. This is what marketers do in advertisements – touch emotional chords so you remember their product. What I will do in this book is enable you to make that emotional connection with others – friends, family members and business associates – through effective communication.

In addition, this book will illustrate in many stories just how mastering the art of effective communication can also ignite a series of positive repercussions...something I call the "ripple effect," just like Tim Gard did for me. In addition, I will provide you with some base skill sets to enable you to become a master communicator so you can reach out and connect with and for people, and in turn ignite a ripple effect that touches not only many others but leads you to the success, prosperity and mastery you desire...*and, most importantly, deserve.*

Reach Out FROM Steve

Maximize the Value of this book

Would you like to receive even more benefits from this book?

Yes? Then take 2-3 minutes to watch author Steve Gavatorta *REACH OUT TO YOU* with details of his Top 10 Nugget List.

The Top 10 Nugget List will provide you with a roadmap to maximize your success as a master communicator.

To watch Steve's message, simply go to the following website:

www.reachoutapproach.com/nuggets

Reach Out TO Steve

Reach Out and Connect - Ask a question, interact and share

Is there an important question you want to ask or gain clarification on?

Do you want to share a story or a "win?"

Do you want to interact with other master communicators?

Yes? You too can *REACH OUT TO STEVE AND OTHERS* at the following website:

www.reachoutapproach.com/communicate

THE REACH OUT APPROACH

The purpose of the story in the introduction and of this book is to illustrate what a long lasting and powerful impression that a simple gesture to *reach out* can have on people and relationships. The subtle gesture by Tim Gard resonated with me so much that I speak about it when I train people on the art of effective communication. His approach tied right into what I am most passionate about and what I help my clients with every day. In fact, I call this the Reach Out Approach. Simply put…

The Reach Out Approach is a communication process for initiating, developing and leveraging mutually rewarding relationships

In this book I will help you leverage the Reach Out Approach in your lives so you can achieve the success, prosperity and mastery you desire… *and, most importantly, deserve.*

A POSITIVE RIPPLE EFFECT

Again, a subtle effort to reach out and communicate with me has touched thousands of lives. If that is the case, just imagine what broader concerted efforts to connect can do for people. Just imagine if you could master the art of effective communication and what that could do for you and those with whom you interact. This ability to connect affects everything we do and everyone we interact with on a daily basis – we have the ability to connect and touch lives every day and, in turn, set forth a flow of positive repercussions to hundreds, maybe thousands, maybe millions of people – what I call the "ripple effect of effective communication."

The same way a rock when thrown in the water causes a ripple effect, so can you cause a ripple effect in the lives of others. Sometimes it can be negative, sometimes positive. The point of this book is to empower you to create positive repercussions or ripple effects, not negative ones. When we reach out and connect with people, we create positive ones, but when we don't or disconnect we can send a negative one. So realizing the sheer power of that, doesn't it make sense to raise our awareness and take the initiative to reach out and connect? The key point to know is that we can control the ripple effect by following the process within this book.

PERSONAL AND PROFESSIONAL BENEFITS

The ability to reach out affects our lives personally and professionally. Whether it is at home, in a work environment or other situations that arise every day, our ability to successfully reach out and connect is directly correlated to our success. The more effective and successful we are at connecting through communication, the more successful we will be in any area of our lives. Just think about the following examples:

- **Personal Relationships** – By reaching out and connecting our personal relationships will be deeper and more meaningful.

- Intimate Relationships – In any intimate relationship, the better you connect the more meaningful and in depth the relationship becomes.

- Parenting – The better you can connect with your children, the more rich and rewarding the relationship will be.

- Friendships – The better you connect, the more friends and closer friendships you will have in your life.

- Community – The better you connect the better relationships you'll have in the community.

- **Professional Relationships** – By reaching out and connecting our professional relationships will be much more productive and rewarding.

  - Sales – The more you can connect with your clients the more sales you'll close.

  - Customer/Client Service – The more you can connect with your customers the higher their customer satisfaction and the more successful your business will be.

  - Managerial Effectiveness – The more you can connect, the more effective manager you will become.

  - Leadership – The more you can connect, the more effective you will be as a leader.

  - Team Dynamics – The more you connect with others, the more productive team member you will be and the more effective the team will be as a whole.

- Entrepreneur, Business Owner – The more you can connect, the more successful your business will become.

- **Situational Dynamics** – By reaching out and connecting, we will be able to effectively handle an array of situational developments that arise in our lives on a daily basis.

  - Change – The better you can connect, the better likely you will be able to adapt during changing times.

  - Conflict – The better you can connect, the more astute you will become at avoiding unnecessary conflict and maneuvering through unavoidable conflict.

  - Negotiations – The better you can connect the more effective you will be at negotiating, whether it be a business deal or differing factions of people, your ability to connect is of the utmost importance.

So to summarize, the benefits of reaching out and connecting are huge, basically having a powerful influence on nearly everything we do and everyone we come into contact with. Whether you are a sales rep trying to close sales or a leader trying to motivate a team or a parent trying to connect with your child, doesn't it make sense to be proactive and proficient in this arena?

The point here is that human interaction is a part of nearly everything we do in our lives. To neglect focus and growth in that area is detrimental to our development as people and robs us of the rewarding relationships and success we desire and, most importantly, deserve.

The purpose of this book is to help each one of you become better at reaching out and connecting through effective communication and human interaction. I am not just speaking about a one-on-one dialogue or an email or text message. I am speaking about a relationship where there is a truly meaningful connection that transforms and changes lives in the positive – again both personally and professionally. I firmly believe that we are, indeed, losing the art of effective communication and that this art will be a differentiating point for our personal and professional success. And, even more so in the future.

THE REACH OUT APPROACH: THE BASICS OF EFFECTIVE COMMUNICATION

What do I mean by the Reach Out Approach? There are various definitions of effective communication. I am not merely speaking about sharing a message and information back and forth. I'm not speaking of emailing or text messaging. What I am talking about is making lasting impressions, reaching out and finding common purpose and planting the seeds for long lasting meaningful relationships – touching emotional chords. As defined earlier in this chapter, the Reach Out Approach is a communication process for initiating, developing and leveraging mutually rewarding relationships. The Reach Out Approach is also:

A People-Centric Approach

By "people-centric approach" I mean putting your focus on people by making the effort to understand how people relate, communicate and in turn make an effort to reach out and initiate a connection. This is about finding ways to reach others at a powerful level beyond meaningless dialogue by understanding those with whom we interact and communicating in a manner meaningful and receptive to them. This

THE REACH OUT APPROACH

includes tailoring our communication to better match theirs. This also includes people who are even introverted and shy. Even shyer, introverted folks can learn to better communicate and connect with others as well. You'll learn how to in this book.

THE REACH OUT APPROACH, A CLOSE CORRELATION: PEOPLE-CENTRIC AND CUSTOMER-CENTRIC MODELS

The people-centric Reach Out Approach is a similar approach used in the popular solution-selling model in the world of sales. The solution-selling model focuses on a customer-centric approach meaning that the key to closing a sale is to understand your customer's needs first and foremost. You first find out the issues "keeping the customer up at night" and then solve for that problem with a capability that you offer.

The premise behind the solution-selling model is to not just sell them anything you can or everything that is in your product line. The point is to sell them something in your arsenal that is tailored, specific to them that in turn solves the problem keeping them up at night – hence customer-centric. Once a sales representative is viewed by their customer as customer-centric and providing solutions, he/she is no longer viewed as just another vendor trying to "sell their stuff" but instead is viewed as a trusted business advisor providing solutions. The value of this sales representative just grew exponentially. In addition, they have successfully differentiated themselves from the competition.

The people-centric approach of Reach Out communication is the same philosophy. It is about realizing a connection and seizing it. The difference is that, in the people-centric Reach Out Approach you learn the communication dynamics of those with whom you interact and connect with them in that manner. In other words, you learn about them and how to connect and tailor your approach accordingly.

In the story I told about Tim Gard he simply expressed a subtle realization that I was being shut out of the conversation. He knew how uncomfortable that was for me and he acknowledged it with the subtle hand to my shoulder. He was being conscientious of me and how I felt – that is people-centric. It is also what the Reach Out Approach is all about.

SUCCESSFUL PEOPLE REACH OUT TO MASTER THE ART OF EFFECTIVE COMMUNICATION

I firmly believe the successful people I've known and most admire are people-centric and have mastered the art of effective communication through reaching out and connecting. One of the best I've seen was a former VP of sales in a company I once worked for. He was a very intimidating man. He was intelligent, confident, well spoken, big and imposing. People were naturally intimidated by him. However, he had a gift for making people feel comfortable around him. In fact, at meetings when he spoke, he would always start with some self-deprecating humor to put us at ease. And it worked. With a short, funny, subtle story he could move the room to stitches and help everyone relax. In an unselfish way, he owned us! We would run through walls for him. He was one of us and he felt our pain. In addition, it also built trust, loyalty and respect. As I said, he was a confident man, but didn't let his ego drive him because he was people-centric. He was able to turn our fears into dedication because he knew how to reach out and connect.

Let me provide three examples from ordinary people who came from very humble roots to become great leaders, motivators and communicators primarily because of their people-centric approach and ability to reach out and connect.

Vince Lombardi, perhaps the greatest professional football coach ever, was asked about his approach to his players, specifically, how he critiqued them. His response was as follows:

> *"You can't coach without criticizing, and it's essential to understand how to criticize each man individually. For instance, some can take constructive criticism in front of a group, and some can't. Some can take it privately, but some can only take it indirectly. Football is a motivation business, and on my teams I put on most of the motivation. The point is that I've got to learn forty ways to motivate forty men."*

This quote illustrates that he clearly knew each one of his players was unique and different in their own ways and how they would respond to criticism. It was incumbent upon him as the coach to identify the factors that motivated each one of them and reach out and approach them in that manner. Because he took this approach to reach out and connect, he had great success as a coach and was revered by his players, even the ones for which he had high expectations and made huge demands. He was beloved even by these players because he clearly understood the ways to reach out and connect with them. His tough love approach worked with some, other players it may not and he knew it and adjusted accordingly.

What was the ripple effect of Coach Lombardi's people-centric approach? His teams won five NFL championships including two

Super Bowls. His overall record was 105-35-6 including a 9-1 record in the post-season. He may have won many more if he hadn't passed away at the height of his career from cancer. He not only developed great players, but great men who had successful, productive lives after football. Not to mention the millions of fans who have fond memories of watching perfection in the game of football.

Barry Alvarez, another highly successful football coach at the collegiate level subscribes to a similar philosophy. The story of Coach Alvarez and his success at turning the University of Wisconsin football program from lowly loser to perennial powerhouse is legendary. Not only was the turnaround a success, but the speed by which he did it was stunning. In just his fourth year his team won the Big 10 Conference with a winning record of 10-1-1 and the schools first ever Rose Bowl – the first of three Rose Bowl wins!

You see, Coach Alvarez is a people person and subscribes to a people-centric approach. He knows how to reach out and connect with his players and it starts while he is recruiting them in high school. In his autobiography *Don't Flinch*, Coach Alvarez says:

> *"Everybody is different. And your sales pitch has to change accordingly. You can scare off some recruits by being too aggressive. Yet there are times when you need to be aggressive if you're not getting much feedback."*

Now, once Coach Alvarez successfully recruits these players his people-centric approach continues when they arrive on campus. Here is some wisdom from Coach Alvarez regarding his coaching approach to his players:

"You have to have a feel for your players. I think that's one of my strengths as a coach, and always has been. You have to know what buttons to push; when to push them and when to back off."

Coach Alvarez uses a similar approach as Coach Lombardi – tailor the approach to each person individually – in other words, learn to adapt the style based on the player. The ability to communicate through connection with each player individually is what differentiates the good coaches from the great ones. In fact, if you look at any sport, the successful teams are those where there is strong connection amongst the players and coaching staff. This same philosophy holds for businesses, and any personal and professional relationship.

What was the ripple effect of Coach Alvarez's people-centric approach? Coach Alvarez's Wisconsin football teams have a record of 118-74-4. They've won the Big 10 Title three times, the Rose Bowl three times and enjoyed eleven bowl appearances with an 8-3 record – again after years and years of losing seasons. In addition, he has a high graduation rate and his players go on to lead productive lives – many land in the NFL. And lastly, the positive PR and pride that has come to the school creates enthusiasm in the student body and encourages alumni to donate money and time which, in turn, affects the many lives of the students, both current and future. And for Coach Alvarez, a personal ripple effect, as he was promoted to Wisconsin's Athletic Director where he can reach out and connect with all the athletes and in turn have a broader impact on the school. The ripple effect is endless!

The *Tampa Tribune* recently featured an article about Florida Football coach Urban Meyer entitled "UF's Meyer a Master Motivator." It describes Meyer's approach to motivation. Meyer says in the article, "I think the ability to motivate and understand each individual contributes to the success we had." He adds, "The old adage about treating everybody the same...I cannot disagree more. You have to get to know someone before you can understand how to coach them, how to treat them, how to get the most out of them." Meyer's short record as head coach at Florida is an impressive 31-8 and includes a National Championship. His overall record as a head coach is 70-16, again quite impressive. I'd say Coach Meyer knows what he is talking about regarding motivating his players – his record is an impressive ripple effect of that approach.

Lastly, the same approach was taken by another incredible person I speak about often, Major Dick Winters, who was the leader of World War II's Band of Brothers, as seen on the HBO miniseries, *Band of Brothers*. Major Winters said of his leadership approach:

> *"Sometimes leadership is a matter of adjusting to the individual and you do this every day. You don't have one way of treating people; you adjust yourself to who you are talking to. I might talk to one person one way, someone else another."*

Again realizing we are all unique, he tailored his approach to his men, which in turn enabled them to accomplish feats in the face of adversity no others could ever have come close to accomplishing. Dick Winters clearly understood that each of his men were different and hence tailored his leadership style to match his men. He knew the ones who were afraid, versus "gung-ho." He knew which ones he could push hard and which ones he could not, who he could develop into leaders, and those he could not. He was tuned in to his troops. What made Winters' leadership ability even more impressive is that he was an introverted guy, and actually quite shy. He didn't drink, smoke or curse and spent a good deal of his down time alone. This is interesting as most people think great leaders would be the opposite and more extroverted. But this just illustrates that anyone, any style of person can be a great leader – if they can reach out and connect through effective communication.

Because of his ability to communicate he helped convert a largely civilian army consisting of school teachers, farmers, businessmen – ordinary folks into a force that beat back the most powerful military the world had seen at the time, the German Wehrmacht.

What was the ripple effect of Major Winters' people-centric approach? An incredibly important one as it resulted in helping the Allied armies defeat Nazi Germany and bring freedom to millions. Pretty impressive ripple effect, wouldn't you say?

THE ART OF EFFECTIVE COMMUNICATION AND HUMAN INTERACTION

So as you can see, the art of effective communication goes beyond speaking and talking. It focuses on the art of effective human interaction by clearly understanding others and being able to reach out and connect with them based on these understandings. The ability to communicate and connect also includes understanding communication styles, motivations of others, strengths, weaknesses, how others deal with change, risk taking, conflict and other key factors. The more you can understand the unique attributes of others the more effective you will be in reaching out and connecting with them. So in this book we are going to empower you to master the three-step process of the Reach Out Approach for effective communication and human interaction:

- **Initiate** – Take the initiative to reach out to others versus passively waiting for them. You reach out and initiate by learning how you and those with whom you interact with communicate. This understanding can help set the stage for effective communication.

- **Develop** – Develop the skill of connecting with others by learning to read their communication style.

- **Leverage** – Leverage your communication style so you can engage others at a powerful level *and make an indelible impression as a masterful communicator!*

PRACTICING WHAT I PREACH!

One of the most important things I need to do when working with a client, whether it is a workshop or a speaking or coaching engagement is to reach out and connect. If I do not make the connection in the early stages I may find it hard to connect later.

When I am doing a workshop or speaking, I find the first fifteen to thirty minutes critical in making that connection. In those first fifteen minutes I need to be able to build credibility, relevance and connection. If I do not, I may lose that audience and never get them back. I have seen this happen to many facilitators and speakers who do not connect. The participants don't buy in, get restless and lose interest, and at the worst, get belligerent. When preparing and conducting a workshop or speaking engagement, I walk through the three-step Reach Out Approach process. As an example:

- **Initiate** – In an effort to reach out, I take the initiative to learn as much as I can about my client and the participants. I learn about their business, their industry, their customers, and their competition. I learn about their roles and responsibilities as well. I do everything in my power to reach out to understand them.

- **Develop** – Next, after I've done my research, I develop a plan of action to find areas where I can connect. It may be how the skills I'm training them on can be relevant to their jobs. It may be how a story I share may be relevant to the training or speaking event. It could be finding ways to educate them on things like what keeps their clients up at night and then provide solutions to help them. The bottom-line is that I develop a plan that is based on the research I've done in the initiative phase to in turn reach out and make the connection.

- **Leverage** – Lastly, I engage the audience by having them leverage the newly learned skills to make it relevant to their world. The step of leveraging these skills means getting their investment either physically and/or mentally. By leveraging these skills it also ensures retention that the learning in training will actually be used. Lack of retention in training is a huge problem. This three-step process increases the retention exponentially.

Another speaker friend of mine, leadership artist Dave Timmons, even has a keynote on this topic called "The First 30 Seconds: Rock Their World and Then Some." The focus on this keynote is geared towards other speakers and the premise is that it is imperative to reach out and connect with the audience within thirty seconds. He concludes that if speakers can't reach out and connect within that first thirty seconds then they may not connect at all, and in turn could lose the audience.

The three steps of the Reach Out Approach help me reach out and communicate with my clients and helps ensure the success of the venue, and again, increase retention of learning. In addition, part of my work often includes a behavioral survey so I can get a read on the team dynamics. The behavioral tool, which we discuss in depth later in the book, measures participants on four base behavior styles. Each person's style is determined by how they responded to a short questionnaire. This is useful for me when I am working with my clients. It works perfectly for a team environment when I can get a gauge of the behavior style of the participants and teams as a whole. The dynamics of each team is very exciting because not one I work with is exactly alike. Some teams are a complementary blended mix of all four styles. One may be feisty, gregarious and direct, whereas another may be a quiet, reserved, analytical crew, both examples more of a singular style. The point is, like snowflakes and fingerprints, each group I encounter is unique. That is what makes my job fun, exciting and challenging. No situation I encounter is alike, not one.

The key for me to be successful in my job and to make my sessions practical, relevant and real world, is to use the three-step Reach Out Approach of initiate, develop and leverage. This behavioral tool provides me with a very powerful and accurate way to accomplish that objective.

BECOMING A MASTER!

In this book I will not only further illustrate the need to use the Reach Out Approach for effective communication but also a process to enable you to become a master at it. You see, anyone can become effective at communicating and connecting. In this book, I will supply you with several tools that will empower you in this area. These tools are by no means the only methods, but will provide you with a powerful, relevant and practical foundation to build on. As with coach Vince Lombardi, I am a believer on mastery of fundamentals. We will lay the groundwork for you to be a master of the fundamentals of effective communication.

This simple three-step Reach Out Approach process will provide a solid foundation to help you master the art of effective communication and connection and in turn help you gain the success, prosperity and mastery you desire.

Reach Out Skill Practice

Reach Out Skill Builder Questions

After each chapter, you will be asked several questions so you can immediately apply these techniques to your circumstances.

The purpose is to empower you to become a master communicator by the completion of this book.

These thought provoking questions act as building blocks to help you personalize this information.

It will make them more valuable if you answer honestly and thoroughly.

To take advantage of additional resources go to the Reach Out Approach website at:

www.reachoutapproach.com

Chapter 1 - Reach Out Approach Skill Builder Questions:

1. Do you have a "Tim Gard" story? Has someone used the Reach Out Approach with you?

   • Who is the person(s)?

   • How did they use the Reach Out Approach with you?

2. What was the ripple effect for you?

   • Who else, personally, did this effect?

   • How many others did this effect?

3. Who else do you know that is good at communicating with you?

   • What do they do to reach out, communicate and connect?

   • What attributes do they have that you would like to attain?

4. List five goals you have in reading this book.

Goal #1:

Goal #2:

Goal #3:

Goal #4:

Goal #5:

Introduction & Chapter 1 Notes:

CHAPTER 2

THE CASE FOR MASTERING
THE ART OF EFFECTIVE
COMMUNICATION

P
ersonally, I think the need to master the art of effective communication is more vital than ever. In fact, I think as a society we are starved for it. If you look at some trends it is easy to see; increases in dating services (mainly on-line), chat rooms, and social media sites like My Space and Facebook present prime examples. These are all ways to connect but, unfortunately, I don't think they are delivering the kind of connection that can truly make a difference in lives. In addition, there is a lot lost in virtual connections. Haven't we already heard enough horror stories of people meeting dangerous people online or at least saying that person was not quite who he/she said they were?

WHY AREN'T WE EFFECTIVELY
COMMUNICATING AND CONNECTING?

So why aren't we reaching out and connecting, like we should? I think there are several reasons, but first the more subtle ones:

- **We fear it** – Sometimes based on our styles we may be afraid. Maybe being an introverted person, you hesitate to make the effort. Or, on the flip side, you aren't sure if someone wants to connect. Or, maybe it is a fear to rejection.

- **We don't know we should** – Sometimes we don't realize we should. We get caught up in daily events so we don't. In addition, we aren't aware someone needs us to connect.

- **We know we should but don't** – Sometimes our ego gets the best of us and we refuse to.

- **We don't know how** – In some situations we may not know what to do. In others we just may have a connection deficiency; some people just aren't good at it.

- **We're getting lazy** – Which leads to my next big reason why we aren't...

I believe there are many reasons we are not communicating and connecting with people like we should. Simply put, the 21st Century has ushered in a myriad of changes. That said, we are running faster and harder than ever both in the workplace and at home. The grind of work is getting faster, leaving less time to work on the human dynamic side of things. Unfortunately, the focus on the human dynamic of communicating through connection is placed on the back burner. Several of the following areas are driving the wedge away from making powerful connections.

DOES MORE COMMUNICATION MEAN BETTER COMMUNICATION?

Not all communication is created equal. So I ask, are we communicating for the sake of more communication versus trying to ensure quality communication where there is true connection, the touching of emotional chords? The growth of technology has allowed us to communicate and connect more but:

I firmly believe that much of the breadth and depth of that connection has been diminished because the one-on-one human interaction has been minimized or, oftentimes, been taken out of the equation.

I believe a majority of this technological advancement has been good, but it has been at the expense of one-on-one, face-to-face interactions like the one I had with Tim Gard. That moment with Tim and the positive momentum that took place from that subtle interaction touched many lives. That event would not have happened with a text message. Coaches Lombardi, Alvarez and Major Winters would not have been so successful in leading others if it were solely done via email. It was the human connection that did the trick.

The advancement of technology has been a wonderful thing and has enabled us to communicate more. The question is "Is it meaningful, long lasting connection and does it touch an emotional chord?" If you look at the flow of communication over the years, from phone, fax, email to text messaging it has gradually eroded one-on-one face interaction and chances for the emotional connection.

Now, I am not here to bash technological advancements. Like most of my contemporaries, I text, email and subscribe to a number of social media sites, however, there needs to be a happy medium.

We cannot lose the human side of things. Sitting across a table having a deep meaningful dialogue is significantly better than talking on the phone let alone emailing or text messaging.

Let's take email as an example. Have you ever noticed how email loses some important elements and messages can become misconstrued? Let me provide you with a situation that happened to me.

LOST IN TRANSLATION – MISCONSTRUED MESSAGES

Three years ago, my friend, Tim, set me up on a blind date with a woman named Val. Val and I went to dinner in California. I live in Florida, so it would be a long distance relationship if things clicked with us, but I figured I had nothing to lose. We had a good time. I found her attractive, smart and nice but we didn't get much one on one time to chat and get to know each other. She left and we initially didn't follow-up. Then about a year later, my work took me to California for several weeks. I thought, why not look Val up and take her out for dinner. But the question was, would she even remember me?

Since I did not have her phone number, I wrote her an email that started out "Hello Val, I don't know if you remember me but we met about a year ago…." Her email response began:

"Steve, of course I remember you…"

Then the rest of the message was short, non-descriptive and void of any emotion.

Basically, I could not clearly identify her emotional tone in the email. Even regarding the *"Steve, of course I remember you"* I wasn't sure…

- Was it, of course, "you bonehead" I remember you (anger)?

- Was it, of course, "you hottie" I remember you (excited)?

- Was it, of course, "uhmmm" I remember you (pensive)?

- Was it, of course, "oye vey" I remember you (exhausted)?

The point is that it was difficult to tell the connection via an email. Was it irritation, happiness, nonchalance or pensive? Fortunately, it was the second one (excited!). But again it was hard to tell from the email as it became lost in translation.

As another example, I have a client, a vice-president of sales, who was delivering weekly sales updates to his entire region via the phone. The point was to reach out and keep his entire region up to date on the status of the business. The company he worked for added a new phone system, which minimized his ability to reach the entire region. When he complained that he lost this ability to communicate his message to the entire region, the company said to simply send an email to them. For him, that would not work. As he told me, he felt it was important for his team to hear his voice. To hear the excitement when the numbers were good but to also stress concern for times when sales where down. In other words he lost the emotional impact with email. If you think emails can dilute a message, imagine what a text message does? The point is that he lost his ability to reach out and connect with his region with effective communication.

ARE YOU LOSING YOUR COMMUNICATION AND CONNECTION MUSCLE?

So now the $50,000 question is this: how many times are you using emails, faxes and text messaging methods to communicate in lieu of the one-on-one human interaction? Are you substituting in person, customer calls for a phone call, an email and, worse, a text message? Are your customers saying that is what they need? Are you opting for the quick way out?

If you are becoming lazy and not reaching out to build the one-on-one interaction you may win the battle but you will lose the war, because someone else, most likely your competition will nurture the relationship and make the connection *"face to face!"* Again, email, faxes and phone calls have their place, but I want to challenge you to realize when it is the right place versus when "face-to-face" interaction is needed. I'd bet that reaching out and making that human interaction is needed more often then you may think or you admit.

As an example, I spent many years in sales, both selling and managing sales teams. We always had clients wanting us to fax or email in lieu of seeing them in person. However, we would often find out that our competition was reaching out and getting "face time." In addition they were getting more accomplished with our customers. They were gaining the competitive advantage in many facets – sales, promotions and market share. Why were they? Because they were reaching out and finding ways to get that "face time." They were reaching out and connecting with the customer. This works the same for any relationship, personal or professional that requires human interaction. Phone, fax, email and text all have their place in communication, but not when you need to make the real connection.

CUSTOMER SERVICE? I DON'T THINK SO!

I recently had an experience with a customer service phone call. It was supposedly some company I had an account with, but I really didn't know because their method of connecting was so pathetic it was amazing. Maybe some of you have experienced such a phone call. When I answered the phone, I heard a message saying, *There is an important message awaiting you. Please hold.* I couldn't believe it...a phone call that I didn't even place and then THEY put me on hold? Has the world gone crazy? I never wait; I hang up immediately. This is yet another way to not connect in the customer service world. In addition, it's another example where connection through technology has run amuck. It is no way to connect with your clients, if the darn message is so important, then have someone ready to talk. This is amazing to me...again folks, not a way reach, connect and communicate in the customer service world – not exactly the Reach Out Approach in action, is it?

Reach Out Approach =
Red Carpet Customer Service

Donna Cutting, a customer service expert and author of *The Celebrity Experience: Insider Secrets to Delivering Red-Carpet Customer Service*, says that people are starving for a more personalized customer service. "After having read my book, people will often share their 'customer service pet peeves' with me. I can't tell you how many people complain about constantly receiving voice mail messages directing them to press this button or that button. While this may be easier on the company, it is frustrating for the customer."

A business owner can stand out in the crowd simply by having a live (and lively) person answer the telephone. People like John Wood, CEO of HUB Plumbing and Mechanical, Inc. in Boston, MA, featured in *The Celebrity Experience*, are making red-carpet first impressions by having a real person answer the phone 24/7.

This is partially why they enjoy over 60% repeat business annually.

Cutting says, in this day and age of choosing convenience over your customers, making an effort to reach out and connect in a more personalized way is sure to make your customer feel as if they are receiving the star treatment.

ARE WE EFFECTIVELY COMMUNICATING AND CONNECTING IN THE WORKPLACE?

The importance of effectively communicating and connecting continues to be a big issue in the workplace especially for those of you managing people. Regarding managerial relationships, I recently read an interesting survey in *Training+Development* (T+D) Magazine that was conducted by consulting company Novations Group.[1] The findings really illustrate a significant communication gap between management and employees. The survey asked the question:

Why Does Senior Management Have a Hard Time Connecting with Employees? The results are as follows:

- They rely too much on email   35%

- The assume a single message is enough   30%

- They have no feedback loop in place   28%

- Their message lacks clarity   24%

- *They communicate too much, too often*   *3%*

So the point is that senior management needs to be doing a better job reaching out and communicating with their people. As per the results of the survey, the reliance on email is too much, single messages, no feedback and clarity are problems, and a paltry 3% say their managers communicate too much, too often – maybe a communication gap? I'd say so.

So this survey verifies that there are definite opportunities to reach out and connect in the workplace. Those managers and companies that do will indeed be more successful and in turn differentiate themselves and their organizations. They will have happier employees, which increases performance and optimizes productivity.

To add more to that data and validation to the importance of effective communication, I found the following points in another issue of *T+D Magazine*.[2] The article that captured my attention featured an interview with the dynamic CEO of PepsiCo, Indira Nooyi. When asked "What behaviors and skills must PepsiCo leaders have to implement their operating philosophy of Performance with Purpose," she listed the following five points two of which, **communication skills and coaching**, I believe are relevant to this book:

1. Competence

2. Take a Stand

3. ***Communications Skills***

4. ***Coaching***

5. Your moral compass

So there you have it, communication skills and coaching. It appears that the need to reach out and connect for effective communication is high on the list with PepsiCo as well. Regarding communication, Nooyi says that *"Communication skills are critical. You can never over-invest in them."* Of coaching, she says *"Surround yourself with good mentors. Listen, learn. Your mentor is a major force."* When working with a mentor or coach, you are making a connection with them. When seeking a one-on-one relationship for career advice and in any successful coaching and mentoring environment, communication and connection is key.

So the ability to reach out, connect and communicate in the workplace is still relevant, maybe even more important now than ever. Effective communication skills, the ability to connect should never be underestimated.

"Y" NOT CONNECT WITH GEN Y?

There is another interesting trend that illustrates the strong need to reach out, connect and communicate. This trend has to do with the growth and importance of Generation Y in the workplace.

In fact, I have been very intrigued by articles I am reading on Generation Y (Those people born between 1980 and 1994), also known as Millennials, Echo Boomers and Digital Generation. This group of folks more than any has been brought up in the technological age and most people automatically assume the way they want to interact is solely via technology. Now, that may be true to some extent and maybe because they had greater exposure to technology at a younger age than most of us. But when it comes to work and interpersonal relationships, they desire a close intimate environment where the ability to communicate and connect is vital.

First, let's address a fact that managers are struggling with Generation Y workers entering the workforce. In going to my reliable source again, *T+D Magazine*, I read a recent survey that asked the question and gleaned the following answers.[3]

Does senior management encounter problems communicating with any of the following employee groups?

- ***Generation Y***   ***18.9%***

- Hispanics   8%

- African Americans   7.5%

- Women   7%

- Off-Shore Employees   7%

- GLBT Employees   5.5%

- Older Employees   5%

- Asians   4%

- Physically Challenged   3%

- Recent immigrants   2.5%

- Native Americans   2.5%

- Expat employees   2%

Far and away the problems senior managers have in communicating exist with Gen Y at nearly 19%. The next group, Hispanics, were not even half the percentage. Now that sounds like a big challenge, but not when you learn how to reach out and connect with a Gen Y'er. It actually becomes quite simple. There are two articles that hit the point home that Gen Y folks want to be reached out to and to connect.

In an article entitled, "Connecting with Generation Y", Rebecca Heftner of Novations Group found the following:

"Coaching, openness, collaboration, access, and marketing were the keys to connecting with the most-connected generation." She also listed the following five points as guideposts in interacting with Gen Y:

1. As opposed to traditional mentoring programs where the more experienced manager mentors a younger team member, set up shared coaching sessions. In these sessions the Generation Y team member is asked to talk about what they want in his/her career development. Then the more experienced manager can offer advice that is more relevant.

2. Generation Y team members like to communicate with a manager who has a professional and conversational style. Good posture is important as well as gestures, smiling and eye contact. It is especially important to look at Generation Y team members when they speak. Non-verbally, it is generally better to look open than to look dominant.

3. Generation Y team members place a high value on collaboration and working in teams. They are just as interested in what their peers think as their manager. Managers, who encourage open discussions, peer learning and plenty of feedback tends to attract and retain Generation Y team members.

4. Generation Y team members want to talk and like to be listened to. Long presentations with little opportunity for interaction and "death by PowerPoint" have limited appeal. For the Gen

Y'er, it is best to save large amounts of detail for the company intranet or email where they can access it 24/7.

5. Be prepared to clearly explain why working for the organization is fun and provides work life balance. The benefits of working for the company need to go way beyond the healthcare package. The benefits should include open door policies, community involvement, training for current future positions and mentoring programs. Just as important, if the Gen Y'er tells you they want to leave because a new job opportunity has more variety listen patiently and keep in touch. Generation Y team members may want to return if their transition out of the organization was handled positively and respectfully.[4]

A second article entitled "The Arrival of the Next Generation," states that "This new generation will require a different kind of management, one that is encouraging, motivating, gentle and personalized. The Millennial want a coach that not only guides their efforts, but provides a role model as they reach for career goals. They are focused on their achievements and growth, and won't settle for unappreciation and stagnant positions. This generation knows they have options and are in search of that dream job, expecting to come close."[5]

I think there is a perception that Gen Y prefers to do almost everything online. That may be true to some extent, as they were the generation raised in this technological era. But, Gen Y folks are indeed human. They are not robots. In addition, I think the data above validates the need and method on how to communicate with them. It sounds to me like Generation Y, despite growing up with technology is requiring more communication and deeper emotional connection than other generations. This sounds counterintuitive based on their advancement with technology and their role in it but it's hard to argue with the numbers.

The point is the need to reach out and connect for effective communication is stronger than ever and a very hot topic with the newest group entering our workforce. Are you prepared to reach out and connect with them?

MASTER THE ART – SET YOURSELF APART

So there you have it. It is more vital now to reach out and connect for effective communication. Those organizations and individuals that can become people-centric and master the Reach Out Approach for effective communication will succeed now and in the future. By reaching out, connecting and effectively communicating you will differentiate yourself from others. Your personal and professional relationships will be significantly richer and rewarding, which in turn means better things for you.

In the next chapter we'll begin investigating ways you can reach out and connect. Specifically, we'll review the Reach Out Approach three-step process to help you become a master communicator.

Chapter 2 - Reach Out Approach Skill Builder Questions:

1. Are you reaching out and communicating with people in personal and professional realms?

    - If so, how?

    - If not, why (fear, don't know how, reliance on technology)?

2. Are you over-utilizing technology in lieu of human interaction?

    - If so, how?

    - What can you do to reach out versus relying on technology?

3. Think of someone personally or professionally that you should be reaching out to but have "difficulty" communicating and connecting with them?

    - Who is this person?

    - Why should you be reaching out to this person?

- Why are you having "difficulty" communicating and connecting with this person?

- What are the benefits of reaching out, communicating and connecting with this person?

Chapter 2 Notes:

BRIDGING THE
COMMUNICATION GAP

I hope that you now realize the importance and benefits of the Reach Out Approach. And I am speaking of more than the obvious benefits to you, like success, prosperity, mastery and peace. This includes the benefits of those with whom you are connecting as well as the ripple effect it has on all others thereafter.

There are many ways that we can reach out, connect and communicate. As we discussed in the previous chapter there are several reasons we do not. I can't answer the reasons why you personally do or don't, but what I can do is provide you with a way and a skill set to not only do it, but become good at it. I firmly believe that knowledge is power. I am of the belief that the more people know about something, the more comfortable they are about using the information.

FOUNDATIONS AND BUILDING BLOCKS

This is the reason why anyone who wants to master something practices at it. The familiarity with the subject builds confidence that in turn improves results. In addition, once certain skills are learned they can act as building blocks for next steps and more complex things. This is actually common sense knowledge that we learned in grade school.

Why did you do homework? Work on math problems? Learn to conjugate verbs? They were all critical steps you had to learn to help you gain confidence in your knowledge to then go to the next step. Essentially, they all set the stage for future learning. This is the reason why sports teams, musicians, actors and dancers practice. Anyone that wants to become master and expert in their field of endeavor practices.

This same process can help you become better at reaching out and communicating. If you look at the previous chapter's reasons why we aren't reaching out, many can be resolved by simply knowing how and when to reach out. That is what we will work on going forward, providing you with a foundation to effectively connect and communicate by applying the Reach Out Approach. Once the foundation is in place and you gain the knowledge you need, you will become much better at it. We will provide the foundation, which builds skill sets and confidence to master the art of communication.

BUILDING THE FOUNDATION FOR EFFECTIVE COMMUNICATION - THREE SIMPLE STEPS

As I said earlier, the Reach Out Approach consists of three steps. These three steps provide the foundation for mastering the art of effective communication.

Step #1 - Initiate: Now you may ask, will this work? I say a powerful, affirmative, YES! Do you know why? Because I see it come to fruition in my workshops, speaking and coaching engagements. The key to the first step revolves around two key points:

The first point is enabling people to become better at initiating by teaching them to first understand base behavior/communication styles.

We will speak more about the base communication styles in this chapter and remainder of the book. It is imperative that folks realize people are different and know exactly what their differentiating points are. This knowledge will give them courage to take initiative and take the steps to reach out to others.

The second point is self-knowledge. I help people better understand themselves based on the four communication styles. When I speak of behavior/communication styles it involves many facets – how they behave, communicate, what motivates them, what their strengths and weaknesses are, how they deal with change, risk taking and conflict, among other indicators. If we don't have a good introspective look at ourselves first, it is hard for us to effectively initiate contact and to connect with others. You would be amazed – or maybe not – at how many folks are not introspective and not aware of themselves let alone how they interact with others. Once that introspective acknowledge-ment takes place, we move on to understanding others, which further provides us the courage to initiate.

In my sessions, this introspective understanding is a huge "a ha" moment. It is enlightening and insightful for people to understand why they do what they do. In addition, I find nearly all people excited to learn a bit about themselves. Aren't you? I know I am. I am on a life mission of self-improvement and the first step in this process is self-awareness. This self-awareness provides a baseline to build from and provides insights to become better at making decisions as well.

In fact, this introspective knowledge, using the model in this book, gave me the strength and courage to start my own business cold turkey. It gave me the courage to pursue my dream of starting my current busi-ness. I didn't have the courage to do it until I really learned more about myself, my style – what drives and motivates me, what my fears were and what my strengths were. This self-knowledge provided the foundation or base to take the risk and follow my dreams. So, again, does this process work? Yes, I can attest to that from my personal experiences and from those of the clients I see in my sessions.

Step #2 - Develop: Once that foundational step of self-knowledge or learning about yourself is complete then we move onto learning about others to better develop the connection. The point of this step is to learn about how others communicate. In other words, what is their communication style, how do they connect with others? Then taking the introspective knowledge about yourself to identify and develop any connections between you two, you can begin to gauge how you can connect because that will enable you to leverage the relationship for effective communication.

Step #3 - Leverage: Then the final step is learning to engage with others by learning to adapt and leverage your approach to communicating so it resonates with them. To help you understand this further, just think about the examples provided in Chapter 1 – Coach Lombardi, Coach Alvarez and Dick Winters. They are prime examples of people with self-knowledge who also have the ability to read others. These two attributes allowed them to initiate an approach based on reading other people's styles and developing the connection that enabled them to leverage the relationship. By leverage I mean to have a deeper, more successful level of communication.

Before we delve deeper into the three steps of effective communication, the first thing we need to do to bridge the gap is realize we are different. We are all unique people and so the way we communicate and receive information varies. To become effective as a Reach Out Approach communicator, this point is imperative to remember. Once we realize that we are unique and different, we'll realize that our communication styles and the way we connect is unique to us. We realize that to make connections we've got to bridge the gap from how we communicate to how others communicate.

DNA, FINGERPRINTS AND SNOWFLAKES

Most of us, when communicating, tend to speak from our point of view without truly understanding someone else. The beauty of the Reach Out Approach is that it puts other people first – remember, it is a people-centric approach. It also involves empathy, or understanding things from someone else's point of view.

You see, we are all different and very much like snowflakes. We all have DNA and fingerprints unique to us. So wouldn't it make sense that the way we connect and communicate varies by individual as well? We have similarities, but I think we don't give justice to others when we fail to consider the unique differences and make an effort to acknowledge it.

Now when I speak about the differences in the way we communicate and connect, I am speaking more than just to the unique conversational aspect. I'm speaking of many facets that encompass our being – what motivates us, how we respond to change, risk taking and conflict. Basically, I am speaking about the following points:

- How do we communicate in general?

    □ Are we forceful, challenging and ambitious?

- Are we talkative, friendly and expressive?

- Are we steady, relaxed and methodical?

- Are we analytical, contemplative and careful?

- What is our communication style?

  - Are we straightforward?

  - Are we friendly and informal?

  - Are we warm, open and sincere?

  - Are we logical and detailed?

- Are we more extroverted or introverted?

- Are we more people-oriented or task-oriented?

- Are we direct or indirect?

- What is our propensity to deal with change and take risk?

  - Do you love or fear change?

  - Are you a big risk taker or afraid of risk?

- What is our conflict response?

  - Do you fight, run, tolerate, avoid?

- What are we gifted in?

  - Getting tasks accomplished?

- Persuading others?

- Solving people problems?

- Analyzing task and procedures?

- What are we motivated by?

  - Challenges?

  - Image?

  - Peace, stability?

  - Excellence, quality?

- What is our ideal environment?

  - One with challenges?

  - Open, flexible and fun?

  - Helpful, no conflict?

THE REACH OUT APPROACH

These are just a few questions to know about yourself and those people with whom you interact. The key point in the Reach Out Approach is first understanding yourself and then understanding others so you can leverage the relationship for mutually rewarding purposes. If we have a good understanding of how we would answer these questions and then in turn how others would, then we could be much better at interacting with others. Once we can answer such questions about ourselves and others we can truly connect. As illustrated in the following graph, we can find common ground where the connection exists.

The Reach Out Approach

Communication Style

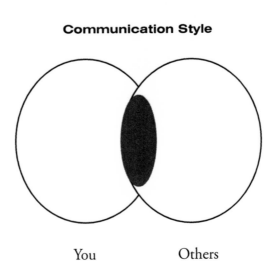

You   Others

A FOUNDATIONAL TOOL FOR YOU

For years I have conducted workshop training on the topic of communication skills. The basis behind the workshop is three-fold:

- Understand your communication style (Initiate the Understanding)

- Learn to read the communication style of others (Develop the Connection)

- Adapt your style for effective communication (Leverage the Relationship)

The tool that I have found most effective in building this valuable skill set is a behavioral model called DISC. This behavioral model is built from an assessment survey. There are many good assessment tools that can identify behaviors and personality, but I have found this tool to be the most valuable for several reasons. DISC is:

- Observable – Meaning you can observe the behaviors in action

- Universal – Meaning these four base styles are recognizable anywhere around the globe

- Practical – Once you learn about this tool you can use it immediately

- And most important, it has an 85% predictive accuracy – it is a highly accurate predictor of behavior

To explain this behavioral tool more in depth, when people take this assessment survey they will receive a score across four behavior styles. The D, I, S and C represent an acronym for the four styles – We will learn about each of these in depth on the following four chapters. But the words associated with the DISC are as follows:

- D = Dominance

- I = Influence

- S = Steadiness

- C = Compliance

The scores across each of the four styles range from 0 to 100. Any score above 50 represents a highly observable behavior. As an example, one of the words to describe a High "I" or Influence style is talkative. So if someone scores 50 and above on the "I" scale they will be talkative. The key to realize is the higher the score the more pronounced the behavior will become. So someone with a score of 95 is much more talkative than someone at 60. When you take the assessment it will give you a score across all four of the styles.

The key to note is the highest score is called the Primary High Style or the most observable behavior and communication style. Any other style above the 50, which is not, the Primary High Style is called the Secondary High Styles. The importance of Secondary High Styles takes precedence the further up from the 50. Someone may exhibit three styles above the 50 mark, which means they exhibit a bit of all three styles. However, the most predominant observable behavior is the one with the highest. And again, the higher the score from the 50, the more pronounced the behavior and communication style.

As an example, if someone has the following DISC score:

- D = 33

- I = 55

- S = 74

- C = 62

The person's Primary High Style is "S" because it represents the highest score (and farthest above the 50). Then the Secondary High Styles are the "C" and "I" because they are also above the 50. But out of those two the "C" would take precedence over the "I" because it is the higher score (and farthest above the 50 mark – other than the "S").

Now you may be thinking, didn't Steve say to look at everyone as individuals – DNA, fingerprints and snowflakes? So why now is he categorizing us in four buckets? Yes, I did emphasize our uniqueness, and that is of the utmost importance to remember. However, I also don't mind using an accurate and proven tool to help me get a fairly quick and accurate snapshot as to someone's behavior and communication style. This allows me some guideposts for making connections and this behavior model enables me to understand people rather quickly – to make that first effort to connect. Again, it is simply a first snapshot and if correct, which most often it is, I follow the lead. In addition, please remember the breadth and depth of the style differences. This includes the breadth or "blend of styles" represented by scores above 50 and the depth of styles or how high above 50 the style is located.

BEHAVIOR AND COMMUNICATION 101: BACK TO THE BASICS

Simply put, this tool provides me with a powerful foundational element for understanding people. Any time where I've been successful in my life, I had a clear understanding of its foundational element. Whether it be the foundation elements of reading, writing and arithmetic or the 4 P's of marketing or blocking and tackling in football, the DISC behavioral tool has provided me and my customers with an excellent tool for understanding people and hence learning how to better communicate. Now, there are many good tools for assessing behavior and personality styles in people. Examples may include, Myers-Briggs or Social Styles. I just happen to prefer DISC because of its simplicity, accuracy and practicality.

Now, before I move forward, I want to make a few important points:

There is no right or wrong behavior style – Often these types of assessments gain a bad reputation because of the method by which they are administered and taught. As an example, they can be used to pigeonhole people. I have heard people say *"because you are a certain behavior or personality style you could never be....a manager, leader or whatever."* This is NOT how I use this tool or how it should be used. Yes, it will give indicators of how someone may do in a certain scenario or job function but it isn't the end all. Who am I to tell someone they cannot be a leader based on their DISC style? It will give me insights into what I can do to help that person become an effective leader, which is how I use this tool.

In addition, I come from the point that anyone, any style can become effective if they can leverage their style by connecting. The basic premise of this tool is that if we can know our behavior styles and connect we can become effective communicators – essentially bridging the gap. That is the key and why I use this tool for reaching out and communicating.

> *You don't need to take the survey to initiate (learn),*
> *develop (read) and leverage (adapt).*

Oftentimes, I am asked in workshops, Steve, this is a great tool, but how do I learn other people's styles without them taking the survey?

What I do is teach people how to read the styles through observation. We will do that in this book. Folks do not need to have others take the survey to become good at communication. It helps, but is not necessary. In this book, I'll teach you the valuable and practical skill set of reading others.

YES, WE ARE UNIQUE – BUT HOW ABOUT A SNAPSHOT?

As I mentioned, the premise behind this behavioral model is that there are four-base communication styles and each of us exhibit at least one of them to some degree. The key though is that we are actually a blend of the four styles. There is, however, a breadth and depth to each person's style as well. This adds complexity to each person and provides that snowflake and fingerprint quality to this tool.

- **Breadth** – As I said, there are four base styles, but based on our unique behavior we can exhibit several. No person can exhibit all four but some may exhibit three, some two and even one. The point is each of us have different blends of the behavior styles.

- **Depth** – In addition, each style varies in the strength and power of its behavioral attributes. As an example, if the behavioral attribute is friendliness, the intensity of it may vary by person. One person may be very friendly and personable. Yet another person may be off the charts friendly, to the point of being gregarious. The point is, again, each person is unique.

As we move forward and help you understand the four styles I will be reviewing them in the next four chapters. To help you better understand, you need to consider that we will be reviewing each one from a pure style perspective. Meaning, we will consider if the person is solely one of these styles alone and no other. The purpose is to help you realize the unique and differentiating aspects of each. Always keep in mind that we are, indeed, often a blend of more than one type.

A SNAPSHOT OF COMMUNICATION BASICS – FOUR COMMON STYLES

Once we review the four styles in Chapters 4 – 7, you will have the tools to take the initiative to reach out. We will then review the steps for reading styles ("developing the connection") in Chapter 8. Then review how to adapt styles for effecting communication ("leveraging the relationship"). Then in the remaining chapters, and actually peppered throughout this book, we will see the three-step Reach Out Approach in action.

So now let's learn about the four styles and, hopefully, more about you and others with whom you interact.

Chapter 3 - Reach Out Approach Skill Builder Questions:

1. Regarding the person you listed in Chapter 2 that you have "difficulty" communicating and connecting with, please answer the following questions:

   • List six to eight words, descriptors and adjectives to describe this person, i.e. aggressive, gregarious, relaxed or analytical. Use words that first come to mind whatever they might be.

   • List whether this person is more extroverted or introverted?

   • List whether this person is more task-oriented or people-oriented?

   • List whether this person is more direct or indirect?

   • How would you say this person deals with change? (Choose which best describes this person.)

      □ Loves change – a change agent

      □ Oblivious to change – doesn't notice

- Cautious - needs time to change

- Concerned – worried about the effects of change

- How would you say this person deals with risk? (Choose which best represents this person.)

  - Loves taking risk

  - Moderate risk taker

  - Moderately low risk taker

  - Very low risk taker

- How would you say this person deals with conflict? (Choose which best represents this person.)

  - Fights

  - Flights, runs

  - Tolerates it

  - Avoids

Note: Please answer thoroughly as we will come back to this exercise in Chapter 8.

Chapter 3 Notes:

REACH OUT AND INITIATE BY LEARNING THE FOUR COMMUNICATION STYLES – THE HIGH D STYLE

Tom was one of my most fast-paced clients. He was a high level manager in the corporate world and was a master at teaching his teams the basics of sales and marketing. The fundamentals he taught his team helped him become known as the top trainer in the company – and the top developer of talent as well.

Tom was a forceful, aggressive and challenging manager. He was direct and very fact based. He didn't mince words and he carried himself well. He was outspoken and very talented. He loved change and to take risks. In addition, he never backed away from a fight, whether it was with internal marketing personnel or upper level management. He was guided by his confidence.

Tom was skilled at taking many data points to build a case for a sale. He had the unique ability to cut through all of the analytics and summarize findings into no less than five powerful points.

Tom had his strengths but at times was known as a bull in the china shop. He actually had a colleague call him a rock eater. Sometimes his directness got him in hot water, but for the most part he was respected by his team and customers for his candor and no-nonsense approach.

I knew that to have my best results with Tom, I had to be prepared. When coaching and making recommendations to him, I had to have my facts straight and had to make my case in bullet-point fashion. He was a busy guy and for him time was of the essence, so the more buttoned up and prepared I was, the more successful my times were in coaching him.

Tom was a typical High D, Dominant behavior style, which is the first behavioral style we will discuss.

> *The Primary High D's basic communication style is straightforward, no BS. You will definitely know where they are coming from as they don't mince words.*

THE HIGH D COMMUNICATION STYLE - DOMINANCE

To help you better understand the styles we will review various attributes which include: words and indicators (which you will learn more about) to describe them, how they deal with change, risk and conflict as well as other interesting identifiers. Please keep in mind that as you review each of these four styles separately the information pertaining to each of them assumes this is the sole "Primary High Style" (i.e. there are no other scores above 50 except the one in which we are discussing in the respective chapter).

Descriptors:

The twenty basic words or as I call them, Descriptors, to describe someone of the Dominant style are as follows:

1. Direct
2. Daring
3. Forceful
4. Innovative
5. Blunt
6. Decisive
7. Competitive
8. Strong-Willed
9. Bold
10. Results-Oriented
11. Domineering
12. Aggressive
13. Goal-Oriented
14. Problem Solver
15. Persistent
16. Demanding
17. Self-Starter
18. Adventuresome
19. Authoritative
20. Inquisitive

Indicators:

In addition to the Descriptors, there are three measures across all four styles that can be used to understand each style better. These measures are called Indicators and they are important as we will discuss them further in Chapter 8:

- The first indicator asks is the style **Extroverted** or **Introverted**

- The second indicator asks is the style **Task-Oriented** or **People-Oriented**

- The third indicator asks is the style **Direct** or **Indirect**

So from a High D perspective, on the first Indicator they are extroverted. And regarding the second Indicator, task-oriented, meaning they would rather work on a task then focus on people situations. It is not that they don't like people, but they are high energy "doers" so they like working on tasks that drive them to finish the work.

Lastly, regarding the third Indicator of directness, they are very direct. You will not need to worry about not knowing where they stand on an issue as High D's don't mince words – you will know.

Simply put, High D styles are gifted in getting tasks accomplished and are very motivated by more authority and challenges. The more tasks and challenges you give them, the happier and more productive they will be.

Change, Risk and Conflict:

Also important is the knowledge of how each of these styles deal with change, risk taking and conflict. Knowing these facts is imperative in connecting with the styles. If you are talking about making a change with a person who doesn't like change, it is important to realize it so you can help them with the process – this means connecting!

High D styles love change and are big time risk takers and will take the initiative during such times. Stagnation will totally bore the High D, so fast paced, changing and high-risk environments are where they will flourish.

With regard to conflict, High D's are fighters; they won't back down easily. The interesting point is that they don't take a conflict personally; it is just how they respond.

Now some other helpful facts about the High D:

Outstanding Characteristics:

1. **Need to Direct** – They have an inherent need to direct and take control of a situation. As I said above, they are basically extroverted people, so they will usually give their opinion in clear specific language. If the group or discussion is moving a little slowly, expect them to step up to the plate and push the group along. Given the authority and responsibility, they can take you to new heights that previously were considered impossible.

2. **Challenge** – Always provide them with a challenge. If a job loses a challenge, expect them to flounder. They must have a continual challenge—a problem to solve, a new challenge, a mountain to climb. If there is no challenge they will take the initiative and create one.

3. **Desire to Win** – They love to win and in their eyes, living is winning. They are driven to win both in the corporate world as well as on the golf course. Vince Lombardi's famous quote, "Winning isn't everything, it's the only thing," is the perfect description of their approach to each situation – personally and professionally.

4. **Direct Communication** – In dealing with people, they will be direct and to the point. No flowery words will be present as they say what they think. They may unintentionally come across as being too blunt to some people who are of other styles. They will take issue if they disagree, even heatedly, but will seldom hold a grudge. As I said above, they will fight, but will not take it personally. After they have spoken their mind, they tend to forget about it – no harm no foul.

5. **High Risk** – They love risk and subscribe to the belief, "the thrill of victory; the agony of defeat." On the downside, they can be a high-risk taker, perhaps not considering the consequences. They will not intentionally try to hurt others, but they do not consider failure an option. Because of the high-risk factor, they need others to supply enough facts and data to make sure the jump is a relatively safe one. Oftentimes, this factor allows them to take you where no one has gone before.[6]

Value to the Team:

1. **Bottom-Line Organizer** – They are very results-oriented so whenever given the authority, they will cut through all the needless steps to get the job done. Oftentimes, the paper pushing activities done in organizations add nothing to the value of the product turned out. Give them the job, set the broad boundaries and they will move mountains!

2. **Self-Starter** – Given a task, the responsibility and authority, they will work long hours to show you they can make it happen. Being self-starters, there is no need to push them to get them going.

3. **Forward-Looking** – They focus on the possibilities of what can happen. They are fearless. Obstacles represent challenges to overcome, not a reason to stop. There is no need to worry as you should expect them to go for the gold.

4. **Places High Value on Time** – They are driven by efficiency: quicker, faster, better. They are interested in how much can be accomplished in the least amount of time. They will speed

up others and the process but expect other styles to resist the change and fast pace.

5. **Challenge-Oriented** – Worrying about a challenge is not even an option they would think about. They thrive on and must have a challenge to be motivated. If there is a challenge, they will take it on. Regardless of how impossible, they will focus all their energies on making it happen. If they are not challenged, they will create one.

6. **Competitive** – They love to win and view winning as everything. Any competitive situation will motivate them to succeed and to perform better.

7. **Initiates activity** – In sports terminology they are the athlete saying "Give me the ball, I'm going to win this game!" They are not one to sit around, remain stagnant and discuss options. They will take the bull by the horns and initiate activity to get desired results.

8. **Challenges the Status Quo** – They are not concerned about the "way we've always done it." They are change agents and will reinvent the old way focusing on one goal – results. They will rock the boat in their quest, and find more efficient ways to get things done.

9. **Innovative** – Being fast movers, they focus on efficiency. This causes them to be constantly looking for shortcuts to get the desired results.

10. **Tenacious** – They are driven to results, challenges and winning. They are forceful and direct. Anything other than winning is

obviously losing so they will be tenacious in overcoming obstacles to reach a goal.[7]

The Ideal Environment for them is one that is fast-paced and where you can provide challenges. Also important are:

- Freedom from controls, supervision and details

- Evaluation based on results, not process or method

- An innovative and futuristic oriented environment

- Non-Routine work with challenge and opportunity

- A forum for them to express their ideas and viewpoints [8]

Possible Limitations

As with all the styles there are downsides. High D's, like I mentioned with my client Tom, can definitely be viewed as the proverbial bull in the china shop so it is important for them to realize how their style can become a negative for themselves and others. Some possible limitations include:

- Overstep authority

- Be too direct

- Be impatient with others

- Be argumentative

- Not listen well; be a one-way communicator

- Take on too many tasks

- Push people rather than lead them

- Lack tact and diplomacy

- Focus too heavy on task [9]

As examples of the downside of a style, in this chapter and following, I will illustrate real life examples of the limitations of each style. **The point of these stories is to emphasize what negative aspects of each style can manifest and if you are that style, what to look out for in your behavior and identify potential disconnects that may occur.** For the examples I will use real situations that I have come to know through my client experiences. Some of you may know these types of people and experienced them yourselves. These examples focus on work related examples, but can also be tied to any personal and/or professional relationship.

"THE BULL IN THE CHINA SHOP"

Lisa had recently taken a job with a small marketing company. At that time she had a brilliant fifteen-year career in several large consumer packaged goods companies. She quickly climbed up the corporate ladder and held many cross-functional job responsibilities through out those years, which included, sales, management, marketing and training – needless to say, she was well versed. She enjoyed her career immensely, but felt she was missing something. Her favorite jobs had really featured her creativity because they entailed fixing something broken (like a poor performing region) or the creation of something new (a new department). She was feeling a bit burnt out and didn't see many opportunities to grow in the current environment. She felt stymied in her growth.

It was at this time she was approached by the small company to start a new department from scratch. Since she was itching for a new challenge in a new environment she decided to pursue the opportunity. The only problem was that the new company had a horrible reputation for its culture and incredibly high turnover.

Lisa, however, liked the woman who was diligently recruiting her. In addition, this woman had a good reputation in the company. So Lisa decided to jump. Almost immediately she smelled trouble as the politics and territorial issues were rampant. To add insult to injury, the company was going through a restructuring and the woman who hired her was moved to another division. And the final straw – the job Lisa was brought in to create was totally eliminated. She had no manager and no job, and this all in a three-week period.

Over the next four months nothing improved as the company tried to find a role for her. She had four different managers in that timeframe. It was the most trying time of her long illustrious career – but nothing compared to what was about to happen.

Through those four months Lisa would continually run into Helen, a high-level vice president in another division. Helen would stop by Lisa's office and make small talk and actually consoled her and provided some advice on how best to manage the situation. Helen also made passing comments about coming over to her division to work for her.

This was quite tempting for Lisa, as she was frustrated, but also for the fact that Helen was a very powerful woman in the company, had decent results and was head of the division most responsible for the company sales volume. The only problem was that she had a horrible reputation and had high department turnover. In addition, some of the comments Lisa heard describing Helen included "wacky" and most interestingly "evil personified!" Lisa, however, felt honored and overwhelmed by Helen's overtures. In fact, Helen offered Lisa an opportunity to work with the team.

It all started off perfectly as Lisa was given responsibility to work a customer base that was previously untapped. People in Helen's department had tried to penetrate this industry to no avail. Helen was very interested in changing that as she came from that industry and saw the potential upside for new sales volume. Lisa immediately worked her magic and soon landed multiple client meetings and garnered significant interest in several of them. She did this all within a two-month period. Helen seemed pleased, and colleagues were shocked at her ability to get meetings. Then all hell broke loose.

About a month later, out of the blue on a Friday, Helen told Lisa she wanted to see her in her office after work. Helen kept Lisa waiting until about 6:30 that evening and then started grilling her on when she was going to close these clients. Lisa was shocked as she just started getting appointments and was in preliminary stages, and besides the close cycle on this business minimally took several months. Not to mention that this was the furthest along anyone had gotten in this industry. She was making headway so the impatience was uncalled for so soon in the process. At this point, Helen gave Lisa a warning that she had better see results soon.

A week later the same story, Lisa barely had a chance to breathe setting meetings, trying to close sales and deal with Helen. Helen became more aggressive and impatient by the day. Lisa was not alone, as Helen's tantrums were often heard throughout the office, berating sales reps with harsh language and "screaming that they were losing the battle!" Helen then turned all guns on Lisa. The initial discussion was a direct, forceful, challenging session where Helen told Lisa she didn't think she could make it and posed the question whether she even cared to make it. It was a total mind game by Helen. Needless to say, Lisa was shocked. The following week, she was on the wrong end side of one of Helen's expletive-laced tirades.

At that point, I began working with Lisa, and assured her it was not her fault and that Helen's behavior was unacceptable and totally ridiculous. We developed an action plan to get her away from this atmosphere and manager who had some anger issues. Although the tirades continued, Lisa regained her composure, realized it was not her issue and placed all efforts into finding new work.

Her resume was stellar; she had great interviewing skills and was soon working with another company and was back on track with her career.

As for Helen, she "turned" yet another talented sales representative and lost another new hire. Because of her aggressive, impatient "bull in the china shop" style she again cost the company valuable dollars of wasted time and talent. She battered her reputation even further and because of her inability to communicate effectively, she lost the connection so important in successful leaders.

TAKE THE BULL BY THE HORNS

You see, instead of the "bull in the china shop" manager, Helen could have been the "bull by the horns" manager. I've interfaced with many effective "bull by the horns" managers, based on the Dominant style. You see, all styles have their strengths and weaknesses. The key to effectively leveraging the style is to realize this fact and emphasize the strengths and minimize the weakness. In this case, Helen didn't leverage the strength of her High D style. And in turn, it continued to haunt her.

REACH OUT APPROACH IN ACTION

To better connect and communciate as a manager and leader, Helen could have done the following:

- Use her fast paced energy to motivate Lisa rather than de-motivate.

- Provide "fair and reasonable" challenges to Lisa and motivate her to reach them.

- Being a risk taker and change agent, help Lisa build programs to close the business.

- Being someone interested in fact based information, help Lisa bring relevant and powerful fact based proposals to the clients.

- Realize that one of her biggest downfalls is her anger and impatience and not to let both of these attributes ruin yet another talented employee's experience with her.

Now, if you are a Dominant Style are you a "bull by the horns" or "bull in the china shop" type? Think about it – whether you are parenting, managing, selling, which are you? And what do you need to do to ensure you're the "bull by the horns" type? The key to remember is that to connect be the "bull by the horns" High D style.

This provides you with the basics on the High D, Dominant Style – To help you identify this style in action, think of people you interface with who represent this style.

Chapter 4 - Reach Out Approach Skill Builder Questions:

1. Do you think you have a High D communication style? If so, why do you think so?

2. Do you know anyone personally who exhibits High D communication style? If so, list them.

   • List what attributes make you think so.

   • Do you communicate and connect well with them?

      ▫ If so, why?

      ▫ If not, why?

3. List five public figures who exhibit High D communication style.

Chapter 4 Notes:

CHAPTER 5

REACH OUT AND INITIATE BY LEARNING THE FOUR COMMUNICATION STYLES – THE HIGH I STYLE

L aura was one of my favorite clients. She was an account manager who also led a sales team. She was excellent at diffusing difficult situations between different factions of people she interfaced with at work. Whether it was internal political strife or disagreements between her sales team and their customers, Laura was the calming force of reconciliation.

Laura was a very outgoing, friendly and gregarious manager. She was always upbeat and always saw the positive in any situation. She was excellent at diffusing arguing factions and was optimistic in the face of adversity. She was a moderate risk taker and change didn't seem to faze her. Although she was good with difficult people, she would rather run than face a fight. She was a very personable and cheerful manager to her team.

She didn't dwell on facts but gathered her energy from being around other people. She had a way of making the angriest customer cool down and become rational.

Along with these strengths came weaknesses. Because she was so people-oriented she tended to trust people indiscriminately. In addition, she was guided by her image of what people thought of her. When times were good and her career was on the upswing, she felt good. When she was in situations where her image was tarnished she responded negatively – it hurt her greatly. This was often where we spent our time working together.

I had my best results with Laura when I appealed to her personality. I never worked with her without first chatting a bit about her personal life. She wanted me to be knowledgeable of every aspect of her life – personally and professionally; that rapport greatly aided my work with her.

My client Laura exhibited typical High I, Influencer, behavior.

The Communication style of a High I is very friendly and informal. They love being with and around others, as they get their energy from people.

THE HIGH I COMMUNICATION STYLE – INFLUENCE

Descriptors

The twenty basic **Descriptors** of someone of the High I style are as follows:

1. Enthusiastic
2. Friendly
3. Trusting
4. Talkative
5. Stimulating
6. Gregarious
7. Persuasive
8. Optimistic
9. Convincing
10. Influential
11. Open-Minded
12. Affable
13. Emotional
14. Poised
15. Popular
16. Charming
17. Confident
18. Generous
19. Good-Mixer
20. Effusive

Indicators

Regarding the three **Indicators**, the first is that the High I style is very extroverted. There will be no evidence whatsoever of introversion. They will not only plan the party, they will host and be the focus of it and ensure everyone has a stellar time.

As expected on Indicator two, they are people-oriented as opposed to task. They don't like working on tasks as it bores them. They gain their steam and energy from people.

Lastly, on the third Indicator, because of their strong people orientation they are also indirect at times. They don't like being direct, especially in dealing with an issue that will hurt other people's feelings. This oftentimes poses problems for them, especially with people that like to be dealt with in a direct manner.

Because of their strength in dealing with people, they are very gifted in persuading others. In fact, they love persuading others to their point of view. As I mentioned with my client Laura, they are very motivated by their image. As I said above this motivation can be a double-edged sword. If their image is positive, they will be motivated and happy. On the counter side, if their image is tarnished, it can be devastating. Many of the High I clients I work with suffer from this dilemma. If for some reason, a "high level" person in the organization is unhappy with them, or doesn't like them or has put a "halt" on career advancement – in each of these situations it has proven very difficult for them. I have run into this dynamic many times. I spend most of the coaching work helping them "re-brand" themselves in the organization to re-build their image and to not be driven by what others think.

Change, Risk and Conflict

Regarding change and risk taking, High I's may not notice change because their emphasis is not on the event of change but the people involved. If change involves people they will be very engaged and concerned about the effects. If not, it may not resonate much. They are moderate risk takers, depending on the situation. Remember, they are people-oriented. If the risk proves helpful to people, their willingness to take that risk will rise and if it might proves detrimental to people that willingness will lower.

Being people-focused, they will flight or run before getting into a confrontation. They are good at reconciling different factions, but that doesn't mean they will engage in a fight, they won't. So if a serious conflict were to arise, they would avoid.

Outstanding Characteristics:

1. **Need to Interact** – Being people-oriented they have an inherent need to interact, and love opportunities to verbalize and communicate. They have a tendency to talk smoothly, readily and at length using friendly contact and verbal persuasion as a way of promoting a team effort. They will consistently try to inspire you to their point of view.

2. **Need to Be Liked** – Driving on their concern of their image, they want to be liked and usually like others, sometimes indiscriminately. They get their energy from people so they prefer not to be alone. They have a need for social affiliation and acceptance. They possess a high level of trust in others and on the downside may be taken advantage of by people. Again driving on the image concept, social rejection is a fear for them. The key to connecting with them is to praise in public and rebuke in private. This is true for most people, but especially this style. They are incredibly optimistic, and excel at building on the good in others and see the positive side of a negative situation. You might say they see the world through rose-colored glasses.

3. **Involvement** – Being very energetic and active, they will be involved in just about everything. At their best, they promote trust and confidence and feel they will persuade people to the kind of behavior they desire. They usually perform very well in situations where poise and smoothness are essential factors.[10]

Value to the Team:

1. **Optimism and Enthusiasm** – Since they have a strong people-orientation, they possess a great ability to motivate and get the team excited. When faced with adversity, the optimism and enthusiasm they exude will keep the team together.

2. **Creative Problem Solving** – They possess a very creative mind and if allowed will be ingenious in their ability to come up with new and creative ideas and solutions to problems.

3. **Motivates Others Towards Goals** – Leadership is the ability to move people toward a common goal. They excel at motivating people through positive interaction and persuasion. This ability causes others to want to work together as a team.

4. **Positive Sense of Humor** – Because of their gregarious attitude they add fun to the team and to the tasks at hand. Studies have proven that productivity is increased as the team begins to have fun. They add that natural fun, humorous element to the team.

5. **Team Player** – Since they need a lot of people interaction, they are a very good team player. They love teams working together because it means having fun while getting the job done.

6. **Negotiates Conflict** – Their strengths with people mean they are a natural mediator. Since they do not like conflict they can verbally persuade both sides to come to an agreement. Part of this is due to their ability to focus on the bright side of the issues. Also, if both factions know the High I mediator, both probably like him/her.

7. **Verbalizes Articulately** – If there is a presentation to be made, an argument to be won, someone who needs to be persuaded into something that is good for all, send him or her in. In these situations they will paint an optimistic picture of the possibilities and have a greater chance of achieving the desired results, not to mention the fact that they will enjoy the opportunity of being energized by the chance to verbalize.[11]

The Ideal Environment for them is one that is open, flexible and fun. Also important are:

- Assignments with a high degree of people contact

- Tasks involving motivating groups and establishing a network of contacts

- Democratic supervisor with whom they can associate

- Freedom from control and detail

- Freedom from movement

- Multi-changing tasks [12]

Possible Limitations

The downside of a High I primarily is over emphasizing their people-strengths, especially with styles that are not as people conscious. Other possible limitations are:

- Oversell

- Act impulsively

- Trust people indiscriminately

- Be inattentive to detail

- Have difficulty planning and controlling time

- Overestimate their ability to motivate others or change behavior

- Under instruct and over delegate

- Tends to listen only in regards to a situation

- Overuse hand motions and facial expressions when talking

- Rely too heavy on verbal ability [13]

THE MUSHROOM MANAGER

Stacy had a manager named Lynn. Lynn was a nice person with a big extroverted behavioral style, a High I. For the most part, Stacy enjoyed working for her by sheer nature of Lynn's people-oriented style. However, it was not enough to outweigh her overall inability to connect with Stacy.

Lynn managed Stacy when she had one of her most challenging clients. They were in an industry where their core business was essentially in decline. Because of growth in technology, they were losing their core business at a very fast pace. In addition, they were re-negotiating a big contract at the same time that had to do with transition into this new technology. If they could secure the new contract it would minimize the business decline, maybe even reverse it.

Stacy's relationship with Lynn started deteriorating rapidly when their styles started clashing. Being a High I, Lynn was constantly shooting from the hip. She was not a planner and accomplished a great deal through sheer use of her personality. It was hard not to like her. However, she was most often oblivious to others' styles and often failed to connect. As an example, Stacy was a style that didn't like changes to tasks thrown on her desk at the last minute with expectations that it be done "yesterday." Now to be sure, in the business world "fire-drills" happen a great deal and Stacy learned to deal and manage it the best she could. But with Lynn it was almost a daily occurrence, and most often could have been avoided. In addition, most of the time it was not necessary and oftentimes she never followed up on it. So most of her "fire drills" were of her own making – either because she didn't want to do it or she, herself, put it off to the last minute. Again, this approach clashed with Stacy and her team and many of her colleagues, Lynn's other direct reports. Lynn was losing the connection with a lot of her team.

As Stacy began building the contract negotiation plan with her team, she needed support and input from Lynn. Some progressive ideas she wanted to implement needed Lynn's approval because it meant an investment in new funding. She needed Lynn's help going to battle for her ideas with internal corporate personnel, especially the finance department. In addition, the customer liked where Stacy's team was heading and was "chomping at the bit" to get moving because her proposal gave them a competitive advantage and they wanted to beat their competition to the punch with a new capability. Lastly, the contract was coming close to ending and Stacy's competition wanted the business badly as well.

So there they were, in a good position to please a difficult client while at the same time change the direction of the business to a more favorable trend. However, every time they tried to get Lynn engaged, she put Stacy's team off. Using her wonderful people-skills to charm Stacy and the customer, Lynn would successfully delay getting involved in helping them move forward. This went on for months and months. It was initially hard for Stacy to get angry at her, because Lynn was so nice and they had originally had a good connection. But as time wore on, Lynn's connection deteriorated with Stacy and the team and most importantly the client. Every time they would get Lynn engaged in the process it seemed like she lost interest again. When asked about getting involved or when they might see some information with some of their requests, Lynn would simply use her bubbly personality to put them off.

Lynn's approach was really taking its toll as Stacy's team started joking that Lynn was a "mushroom manager." For those who don't know what that is, mushrooms flourish by being in the dark and while in manure. A mushroom manager it is said, "keeps you in the dark and feeds you a lot of crap!" That is how Stacy and her team felt about Lynn. Lynn lost her connection to Stacy and her team.

Because of delays and lack of support from Lynn, Stacy eventually would lose the contract and with it a chance to change the direction of the business. Unbeknownst to Stacy, Lynn was having her own issues securing support for Stacy's program. But she didn't want to face confrontation with corporate, Stacy and the client, hence she was leveraging her personality to the hilt instead of forcefully addressing the issue head on. Because of this, Lynn lost the connection with the team and client. Stacy and her team knew her "rose-colored glasses" approach was foolish and it subsequently wore on the client as well. It resonated loud and clear. The fact that Lynn did not reach out, develop and leverage hurt the team and ultimately the company.

It also cost Lynn and the company as Stacy left the company a year later for a leadership role elsewhere and is now actually a highly successful business owner. As in the story of Helen and Lisa in Chapter 4, Lynn's management style cost the company big time – both in the lost contract and business, but maybe most importantly the loss of a strong employee. Again, there is a cost associated with the loss of good employees.

THE MOTIVATOR MANAGER

The "mushroom manager" syndrome is very predominant in the High I style. Because of their friendly, people-oriented nature they don't like confronting difficult situations "head on" and try to leverage their people personality. This may work for a while, but eventually can wear thin. In fact, Stacy who had a great sense of humor, made the funny comment when we discussed "mushroom" manager syndrome. She agreed with that observation and said she felt like telling Lynn she was the "don't pee on her head and tell me it's rain" type person so "mushroom management" would never work with her.

REACH OUT APPROACH IN ACTION

Overall, Lynn missed a great opportunity to be the motivational manager, instead of the mushroom manager. The natural manifestation of a High I style is to be energetic, optimistic and hence highly motivational. Lynn was motivational to some extent, but her unwillingness to deal with adverse and confrontational situations clouded her judgment and approach to the situation. Here's what she could have done differently:

- Use her enthusiasm along with follow up to motivate Stacy, her team and client.

- Use her persuasion skills with internal company personnel so they could provide Stacy's team with the information they needed.

- Act as a mediator between all factions to keep the process going in a positive direction.

- Communicate the status of the situation to all parties – High I's generally communicate well.

- Realize that her biggest downfall as a High I is to be overly optimistic and help the team better manage "real world" expectations with the customer.

Now, if you are an Influencer Style are you a "mushroom" or "motivator?" Think about it – whether you are parenting, managing, selling, which are you? And what do you need to do to ensure you're the "motivational" type?

This provides you with the basics on the High I, Influencer Style. To help you identify this style in action, think of people you interface with who represent this style.

Chapter 5 - Reach Out Approach Skill Builder Questions:

1. Do you think you have a High I communication style? If so, why do you think so?

2. Do you know anyone personally who exhibits High I communication style? If so, list them.

   • List what attributes make you think so.

   • Do you communicate and connect well with them?

     ▫ If so, why?

     ▫ If not, why?

3. List five public figures who exhibit High I communication style.

Chapter 5 Notes:

REACH OUT AND INITIATE BY LEARNING THE FOUR COMMUNICATION STYLES – THE HIGH S STYLE

S tephanie was my most steady and warm client. She was an easygoing manager with her staff. Her thought process was very methodical. She was what I would call the quiet leader. In addition, she had the rare blend of understanding "the numbers" but would always rather interface with people than work on a task.

Stephanie wasn't outgoing or gregarious but had great rapport with people. On a one-on-one level she was terrific. She was steady, relaxed and very non-emotional – so much so, her counterparts called her "even Steven" – an affectionate play on her name. She didn't like fast change as she needed time to feel comfortable with it. Give her time to change and she was fine, but don't force something on her last minute as it was very frustrating. In addition, she was a moderately low risk taker.

Stephanie was excellent at solving problems with people and was fantastic in creating stable, peaceful work environments despite the pressure that may have been brewing.

Despite the stable environment, sometimes her downfall was not addressing issues "head-on" with certain employees and customers. At times she tolerated conflict amongst staff. Her drive for peace and stability often clouded her judgment in adverse situations. In addition, her non-emotional approach was sometimes mistaken as being aloof to the situation.

I knew that to have my best approaches with her was to be very steady and non pushy. The best approach I could take was to provide an environment where she could come to her own conclusions. If I moved casually with her and presented my ideas in a patient manner, I would eventually win her over. It wasn't that she was not a fast learner, she just needed time to gain "a lay of the land" and then she'd be a master at anything she tried. She jokingly said, her life and career mirrored that of the parable "the tortoise and the hare." She may not be the "first out of the box" but she'd eventually win the race. I totally agree with her self-assessment.

Stephanie was a typical High S, Steadiness behavioral style.

The High S communication style is warm, open and sincere. They like interfacing with people and are excellent in one-on-one situations.

THE HIGH S COMMUNICATION STYLE – STEADINESS

Descriptors

The twenty basic words to describe someone of the High S style are as follows:

1. Methodical
2. Systematic
3. Reliable
4. Steady
5. Relaxed
6. Modest
7. Passive
8. Possessive
9. Amiable
10. Predictable
11. Understanding
12. Mild
13. Friendly
14. Serene
15. Good listener
16. Sincere
17. Non-Demonstrative
18. Team-Player
19. Patient
20. Stable

Indicators

Regarding the first Indicator, High S's are introverted, meaning they are not necessarily shy but use their introversion to re-energize. Many High S styles re-energize by being alone. I for one am a High S. So as an example, after a workshop or speaking engagement, I enjoy my alone time. It could be a jog along the water or in a park, or it could be a quiet dinner. The point is, High S styles get their energy back by doing something alone.

For the second Indicator, they would rather interface with people than work on a task. Again, it sounds confusing that High S is introverted yet, people-oriented. Again, their introversion is taken from the perspective of how they derive and re-ignite their energy. Lastly, on the third Indicator, they are much more indirect than direct – mainly for the same reasons as a high I as mentioned in Chapter 5.

As indicated by Stephanie's story, High S's are gifted in solving people problems. They are also motivated by peace and stability.

Change, Risk and Conflict

Regarding change, they don't like it and need time to prepare for it. I myself don't like it initially but once I can gain a "lay of the land" regarding the change, I am normally fine. They are also low risk takers and oftentimes tolerate conflict. When I am working with the High S style I need to help them set boundaries when facing conflict or an aggressive type person. Setting boundaries help them become better at dealing with the conflict and stopping difficult situations from becoming worse.

The other characteristics in understanding the High S style is as follows:

Outstanding Characteristics:

1. **Need to Serve** – They have an inherent need to serve others and help people. They're always the one to help out, in a pinch. They are not selfish and always lend a hand to get the job done. People of the other styles may serve for differing reasons but the High S has a natural tendency to serve. In other words, serving and helping energizes them.

2. **Loyalty** – They are loyal and do not switch jobs very often, preferring to remain in one company as long as possible. They will also tend to stay in a relationship a long time, be it business or personal for reasons of security and harmony. With the goal of harmony, they will become very adaptable to the situation, modifying their behavior in order to achieve a sense of stability and harmony. That is why many are called "even Steven."

3. **Patient, Relaxed** – Because of their non-emotional approach, they show a cool, relaxed face. They are not easily triggered or explosive in nature. Although they are very active emotionally, they do not show their emotion. As introverted people they will hide their problems and do not wear their heart on their sleeve. They've been known to lead their teams to great heights, even while going through incredible personal struggles

4. **Long-Term Relationships** – They will develop strong attachments to their work group, family, club or association. They operate very well as members of a team and coordinate their efforts with others easily. They strive to maintain the status quo, since they do not want change that is unexpected or sudden.

5. **Closure** – Getting closure on anything is essential for them, be it a personal or professional matter. In other words, they must be allowed to finish what they start. To start several jobs and leave them undone is stressful to them. In a task-oriented situation they should be given few tasks and allowed to complete them before moving on. When having to juggle many balls at once, it also proves stressful. [14]

Value to the Team:

1. **Dependable Team Player** – They are viewed as great team players because they are always willing to help out. They usually stay in a situation a long time, as their loyalty has a stabilizing effect on them and others.

2. **Work Hard for a Leader and Cause** – If they believe in a leader and the cause, they will work extremely hard to make it happen

(other styles will also work as hard but for different reasons). They will be quick to assist others in areas they are familiar with.

3. **Great Listener** – Listening skills are a natural behavior for them. Even when interrupted, they will stop and look you in the eye and listen. Great listening ability makes them natural at helping people work through problems. This skill set combined with their logical thinking, they become great assets to have on the team.

4. **Patient and Empathetic** – Combined with great listening skills, they are very patient. They take great effort to really try to understand the situation the other person is in. Sometimes they can become too adapting. They will usually give the other person the benefit of the doubt, and may stay in a situation or relationship too long, hoping that it will get better.

5. **Good at Reconciling Factions, Calming and Stabilizing** – They are driven by a desire for harmony and peace, so they can be a great asset in stabilizing a conflict situation. Again, their patience, listening ability and logical approach can bring them back into harmony and focus.

6. **Logical and Step-wise Thinker** – Getting involved in the planning process, they are great assets. Oftentimes goals are set and the plans to get there are not even thought out. They can bring lofty ideas back to the realm of the real world and point out gaps and flaws in the plan, due to their logical thinking process.

7. **Will Finish Tasks Started** – Closure is of the utmost importance to them. They can, but do not enjoy juggling a lot of balls. A task that is started must be finished. They will finish the first task and then move on to the next. Also having the ability to organize effectively, they will take the initiative to develop a system to get the job done.

8. **Loyal** – When they're on the team they will form loyal, long-term relationships with whomever they can associate. When the going gets tough they may be able to hold the team together because of the close relationships they have nurtured and developed.[15]

The Ideal Environment for them is one that is peaceful, stable and marked by a helpful atmosphere. Also important are:

- Jobs for which standards and methods are established

- Environment where longstanding relationships can be or are developed

- Personal attention and recognition for task completed and well done

- Stable and predictable environment

- Environment that allows time for change

- Environment where people can be dealt with on a personal, intimate basis [16]

Possible Limitations

The downside or possible limitations of the High S focus on the fact that they don't show emotion and don't deal directly with difficult personnel. In addition, they don't deal with changing environments well. Other limitations include:

- Take criticism as a personal affront

- Resist change for the sake of change

- Need help getting started on new assignments

- Have difficulty establishing priorities

- Internalize feelings when they should be discussed

- Wait for orders before acting

- Give false sense of compliance

- Be too hard on themselves

- May stay involved in a situation too long

- Unable to project a sense of urgency [17]

THE RELUCTANT REP

Jeff was a very good sales rep and had a stellar career as one. He had a reputation for having great rapport with clients, which in turn meant he had very few issues with them in his eighteen years of sales. In addition, he showed the rare quality in sales people that exhibit a methodical, systematic approach to sales – meaning he understood sales data and could leverage it very well. That skill, combined with an intuition about people, were keys to his success. He was hard not to like and it showed in his career.

Jeff was promoted to a team leader role calling on one of the most difficult customers in the country. This client had the largest market share in the New York Metro market place and the company's reputation in it was pathetic to say the least. In fact, the previous rep and the client were barely speaking to each other. His company's business was trending down with the client. In addition, the rapport was so bad between that the buying group and sales rep the customer asked the sales rep to be removed from the account.

The company immediately looked to Jeff. How could they lose with Jeff who had the analytic skills the client desired, but also was a great "people-person." He'd win them over in a heartbeat. Well, maybe not quite a heartbeat.

To start the relationship on the right foot and build some rapport, Jeff's manager scheduled a lunch meeting with the client and Jeff. As soon as they sat down, Jeff could feel the tension; you could cut it with a knife. He sat directly across from his buyer, Don, and tried to generate conversation. Immediately Don started grilling Jeff about his experience, or lack there of, in their account. So how could he possibly understand their business? In addition, any question Jeff posed to Don's two managers was responded to with one-word responses – yes and no! Jeff knew from that moment that he had his work cut out. He had some tough customers in the past, but this was to the extreme.

Then just the next day as Jeff put it, "all hell broke loose." Don called him complaining about why their competition had cheaper prices on his products and what Jeff was going to do about it! Don then said he wanted to see Jeff in his office the next day with a proposal to meet their competitor's price. At that point, Jeff barely had his feet wet. How in the heck was he going to build a proposal so quickly? He decided to talk to Don first, and again try to better understand the problem and take another stab at rapport. The attempt landed flat. In fact, Jeff was berated and kicked out of the office for not having a proposal. He was to return the next day with one or else!

As the weeks continued by, Jeff slowly started gaining trust and making "baby step" progress with Don and the account. Unfortunately, anytime any little indiscretion occurred Jeff got a major earful from Don. It became ridiculous as the buyer had his way and Jeff kept "taking the beating" and it was wearing him down. But the die had been cast. Jeff's inability to confront Don to stop the unacceptable behavior set the tone for the relationship. As long as Jeff would not stick up for himself, the more Don felt it all right to berate him. Now by all means, Jeff's response should not have been belligerent either but his toleration of Don's behavior opened the door to the ongoing problems.

Unfortunately, this led to continued bad behavior on Don's part, which in turn began to affect Jeff. Despite his hard work and continued efforts to please Don, for every step forward it seemed took two back. The business actually was beginning to show signs of turning around and actually growing faster than the market. All due to Jeff's persistence, but again the verbal beatings over any issue continued. For the first time in his career, Jeff was losing sleep over his job.

It reached a head when a major issue went unresolved, which was actually out of Jeff's hands. It got so bad Jeff was told he couldn't even come into the customers office with any of his own team.

It was at this point that Jeff hired me to work with him as a coach. He explained his situation and I immediately asked him why he was accepting unacceptable behavior. I made the point that Don's tirades were well outside the boundaries of acceptable behavior and he should not tolerate it. My comments hit him like a "ton of bricks." He said I was right and that he was shocked and disappointed in himself. So what we did next was develop a plan of action to confront Don in a direct manner. The approach was not to be belligerent but to inform Don that his behavior was unacceptable and he could not work with him when he was acting out and being unreasonable. Jeff agreed with the approach but said it would be easier said than done. Being a High S, he did not like confrontation. I then told him to trust me. In fact, I told him that every time Don became angry, that he should be even calmer, more poised.

The next day, Jeff had the opportunity to practice what we discussed. Don called and was on a tirade about some issue. He was yelling and screaming, even using curse words. True to our discussion, Jeff calmly informed Don that he should calm down so they could have a rational discussion. This seemed to anger Don more. Then Jeff repeated himself. Don became even angrier and at that point Jeff began mentally cursing me for making this recommendation, but he kept his cool and patiently requested Don "cool down" so they could talk. Once again Don grew angrier.

It was at this point that Jeff noticed something strange and powerful happen. As he became calm and Don irate, he appeared to get the upper hand and as he became calmer and Don more irate, he felt more in control of the situation. Finally, Don got so angry that he hung up on Jeff. Now Jeff was really mad at me, but he knew I was right. But would the approach work? He would soon find out the next day as he had an appointment with Don.

So the next day, Jeff preparing for the worse drove to the Don's office. I called him on his cell phone and told him to stick to his guns. As he entered Don's office, he saw a noticeable difference, as Don was much more subdued and reasonable. They ended up having a very productive dialogue, a great meeting and set the groundwork for their relationship from then on. It all didn't turn fairytale overnight, but every time Don fell back on his old ways, Jeff responded directly and non-emotionally. A new die had been cast and the situation gradually improved from that point on. A few years later, Jeff eventually left his company for greener pastures, but still calls Don every so often to catch up.

You see, Jeff exhibited a situation that happens to many High S styles. They are very people oriented, don't like confrontation, are low risk takers and often times accept bad behavior. Oftentimes, they simply need to set boundaries. Because he was being the "reluctant rep" he didn't set the boundaries and in turn set the stage that enabled Don's bad behavior to take hold and grow. He could have "nipped it in the bud" by being the Relevant Rep. The weakness of a High S style is to overplay the non-emotional side and tolerate conflict. This trait when overplayed often leads to long-term trouble.

THE RELEVANT REP

So when Jeff was the Reluctant Rep he suffered. Instead he should have become the Relevant Rep, set the boundaries for acceptable behavior in the work environment and make himself relevant. Don's bad behavior simply carried over from the previous sales rep. Jeff has a chance to begin anew, set the stage for a new relationship. He didn't and he initially paid dearly. Because of his reluctance, he became *irrelevant*.

REACH OUT APPROACH IN ACTION

To better connect as a sales rep and team leader, Jeff could have done the following:

- First and foremost address Don's bad behavior in a direct manner

- Leverage his non-emotional style as a positive rather than a negative

- Be more direct with Don, rather than not address issues straight on

- Set expectations with Don, like a partnership from the "get go" instead of letting Don set all of the ground rules

- Realize that one of his biggest weaknesses is to be overly non-emotional at times and not address or tolerate conflict and bad behavior

If you are subscribing to reluctant type behavior, stop it immediately to make yourself relevant. Relevant behavior style ensures you're always "in the game" to connect.

This provides you with the basics on the High S, Steadiness Style. To help you identify this style in action, think of people you interface with who represent this style.

Chapter 6 - Reach Out Approach Skill Builder Questions:

1. Do you think you have a High S communication style? If so, why do you think so?

2. Do you know anyone personally who exhibits High S communication style? If so, list them.

   - List what attributes make you think so.

   - Do you communicate and connect well with them?

     □ If so, why?

     □ If not, why?

3. List five public figures who exhibit High S communication style.

Chapter 6 Notes:

REACH OUT AND INITIATE BY LEARNING THE FOUR COMMUNICATION STYLES – THE HIGH C STYLE

Kim was my most cerebral, analytical client. She was in a leadership role and was one of the most analytically astute leaders I've ever seen. She had the ability to find solutions in any situation by leveraging any facts and figures at her disposal.

She was contemplative, conservative and careful. She was excellent at analysis and using facts, figures and numbers to find solutions for the clients. She was reserved, an introvert, and was always more comfortable working on tasks to find solutions to problems. She was a very low risk taker, was concerned about the effects of change and would always avoid a confrontation.

She had the ability to analyze large amounts of information from various data points and sources. She would then be able to compile this information to present a wonderful coherent story to prove her points and secure the sale.

But her greatest skill was also her greatest curse as she often times suffered from analysis paralysis. In addition, she was highly risk averse so getting her to act on recommendations was often like pulling teeth.

This was also a source of frustration for her manager and interoffice personnel.

To get the best results with her the main thing I focused on was making her comfortable with the changes I recommended and the risks I asked her to take. Minimizing the fear of the change I recommended and removing as much risk as I could was key. Once I could provide the factual reasons for taking the initiative from my recommendations she would be assertive; she did not respond to emotional pleas. As with all High C type people, you must remove risk and ensure they are comfortable with changes. If you cannot solve for those two areas, it will be very difficult to get them to act quickly, if at all.

My client Kim was a typical High C, Compliant behavior style.

The communication style of a High C is very logical and detailed. They are not driven by emotion, strictly facts.

THE HIGH C COMMUNICATION STYLE – COMPLIANT

Descriptors

The basic **Descriptors** to describe someone of the High C style are as follows:

1. Analytical
2. Contemplative
3. Conservative
4. Exacting
5. Careful
6. Perfectionist
7. Accurate
8. Conscientious
9. Evasive
10. Fact-Finder
11. Restrained
12. Precise
13. High Standards
14. Conventional

Indicators

For the first Indicator and like my client Kim, all High C people are introverted. For the same reason on the Indicator two they are obviously more task-oriented rather than people-oriented. And lastly, on Indicator three, they are more direct versus indirect – they don't seek confrontation, but since they are risk averse, they would rather be direct than be wrong, or unsure of something. Again, the reason for this is tied to their risk aversion. Since they are fearful of mistakes and/ or doing the wrong thing, they will be direct and let you know.

High C styles are gifted in analyzing tasks and procedures and are motivated by excellence and quality. They are typical dot the "i" cross the "t" type folks.

Change, Risk and Conflict

Regarding change, they are concerned about the effects. For similar reasons they are very risk averse, low risk takers.

Although they are very direct, they will not seek conflict. In fact, they will do all they can do to avoid it.

Some other helpful facts about a High C:

Outstanding Characteristics:

1. **Need for Procedures** – They strive for a stable and orderly life and tend to follow procedures in both their personal and business lives. Dependent upon procedures, they will usually stick to methods that have brought success in the past.

2. **By the Book** – The first and foremost rule of conduct for them is to "go by the book." They are very aware of and sensitive to the dangers of mistakes and errors, preferring a professional disciplined approach to problem solving. They are often quality people who will write proven procedures to ensure proper outcome.

3. **Perfectionist** – They are constantly striving toward better ways of doing things. There is a right way to do things and a wrong way. They have a desire to be right, which usually means that they will come down on the safe side of a problem, where there is less risk.

4. **Precise and Attentive to Detail** – They are data gatherers and will gather all possible facts (maybe too many) related to a specific problem. They are systematic thinkers, precise and attentive to detail. When called upon by other styles, they will tend to ask questions to clarify the data, and go to the heart of the issue. They are very careful in thought and deed.

5. **Proof and Evidence** – Statements made with little or no proof will not fly with them. Their motto and calling card is "Prove it."[18]

Value to the Team:

1. **Objective Thinker** – When dialoging with them, the real world is the arena. They deal in the arena of objective fact and will make you prove your case. They bring a reality to plans, analyzing and testing the data for accuracy.

2. **Conscientious** – They take their work personally, almost as an extension of their being. The finished task is a reflection of their attention to small details. They are usually very loyal and will go the extra mile to get the job done.

3. **Maintains High Standards** – In a book called *The Wisdom of Team*, one characteristic was found on all high performance work teams...they were committed to the highest standards. They will even assist in writing the standards. With a quality focus, the High C assists the team in consistency of standards and operation, adding order to the scenario.

4. **Defines, Clarifies, Gets Information, Criticizes and Tests** – A great objective thinker, they will blow holes in plans that are not well thought out. Their skeptical nature looks at all possibilities before they buy into a plan. Utilized in this way they can be a great asset to any team. And don't argue with them unless you have your "ducks in a row." Being aggressive collectors of data and information, they are a walking computer, always analyzing, testing and clarifying.

5. **Task-Oriented** – Their work is not all touchy feely, we need people on the team that place urgency on doing tasks that are needed. For years, they have made significant contributions to such events as going to the moon.

6. **Asks the Right Questions** – One of the most significant contributions the High C makes to any organization is asking the tough questions. This talent often leads to detraction of a shallow plan.

7. **Diplomatic** – If given the opportunity, High C's will be very diplomatic in sharing the data to support their conclusions. They prefer discussions void of emotional appeal.

8. **Pays Attention to Detail** – Many projects would be a total disaster if it weren't for the High C's attention to detail.[19]

The Ideal Environment for them is doing things right. Also important are:

- Where critical thinking is needed and rewarded

- Assignments can be followed through to completion

- Technical, task-oriented work, specialized area

- Noise and people at a minimum

- Close relationships with a small group of people

- Environment where quality and/or standards are important[20]

Possible Limitations:

- Hesitate to act without precedent

- Overanalyze; analysis paralysis

- Be too critical of others

- Get bogged down in details

- Not verbalize feelings, but internalize them

- Be defensive when criticized

- Yield to controversy

- Select people much like themselves

- Be too hard on themselves

- Tell ideas as opposed to sell ideas[21]

ANALYSIS PARALYSIS

Andy was CEO of a small consulting company. He was a highly intellectual person and had an excellent formal education, both in the states and overseas. He was smart, very well respected and thanks to his intellect and strong support team, he would always find solutions for his customers by using fact-based analysis from the multiple data sources. He started in a corporate job but left to start his company, at the time a one-man operation. Fortunately, he was able to take some of his current client base with him. This made the transition to his consulting business seamless because it minimized the risk he took by leaving his job and the safety a corporate job offers, especially a sure salary and health benefits. As his business grew, he needed to hire more employees one of which was an office manager.

You see, Andy despite all his intellectual abilities and smarts, was not an effective people manager. To some extent he realized it, but on another side of things it often appeared he didn't even care. To him, what mattered most were "smarts," facts and data. The interpersonal aspect of the business was fine, but if it didn't lead to growing the business it really didn't matter. As the business grew, most of his employees respected him, mainly for his knowledge, but found him oftentimes intimidating and even blunt to the point of being rude. Many in the company oftentimes found his intellect overwhelming, which to some, meant approaching him was intimidating. The business problems started arising when the clients began to feel the same way. His direct, forward approach was beginning to irritate clients as well as his employees. Several clients had left him and "closing" new business was proving more difficult for him.

Even on the social front, people-oriented ventures seemed difficult for him. He was single and appeared much more comfortable alone. He was quite athletic, in fact a tri-athlete and women found him attractive and when he would finally let his guard down, he could be witty and charming.

Even his approach to dating focused more on Internet and social media sites rather than meeting someone in person at a live social event. He felt much more confident chatting online than in person at a party. Although friends and family attempted to set him up, he would either reject the offer or would intellectually dominate his date. He would even appear argumentative if they had an intellectual disagreement. He meant nothing personal but when it came to facts and analytical data, he had to prove his point.

Even women who made blatant direct efforts to interact with him would be brushed off in favor of flirting on-line through one social media site or another – his favorite being Facebook. This left little in the meaning of a nice intimate relationship. In fact, most of those connections involved people who weren't truly the people he thought they would be.

You see, despite his intelligence and success in life, Andy was incredibly risk averse and fear driven. He needed analysis and facts and data to drive his decisions, which is fine but would often lead to stagnation if he didn't have the information at his disposal. Oftentimes, social interactions, both personal and professional didn't supply him with the data he needed to make decisions so he simply avoided them, again opting for a safer venue.

As the years progressed, his company's growth became somewhat stagnant. He had a staff that hovered between sixteen and twenty people but was always in the "interviewing" mode because the turnover was so high. With Andy's style and approach dominating the environment it was a culture that was not people-oriented, fun and, most importantly, risk averse and unwilling to change as the industry evolved. Both the difficult culture and the unwillingness to adapt to the changing environment began to take its toll in the company and, more importantly, Andy. It seemed like a major snowball effect as the business declined and the turn rate increased. Andy became even more protective, risk averse and fearful of change.

In addition, as time wore on Andy suffered from what his staff said was severe "analysis paralysis." They felt he severely hindered their ability to close new business because he felt the need to be involved in every facet of their business. Every proposal and contract had to be reviewed by Andy first before moving forward. He rarely if ever delegated responsibilities to others for fear of errors. He became so overwhelmed it hurt him personally and professionally. He started not enjoying work and had no personal life whatsoever. In addition, his staff was suffering as they could not close any business because Andy hadn't reviewed their work yet. These delays began irritating clients who eventually chose a competitor who could quickly respond to their needs. Andy's risk averse, "dot all i's and cross all t's" approach was having a damaging effect. The biggest complaint was that even when Andy reviewed their work, he would nitpick and send them "back to the drawing board," delaying the response to the client even further.

In interoffice meetings, Andy's direct often belligerent approach was beginning to take its toll on the staff which in turn affected client relationships – this cost them several clients. And it got worse as Andy hated trying to generate new business and despised networking. He even said his innate shyness and unwillingness to approach strangers was a curse.

As the years progressed, the business deteriorated to the point where it was back to being a single person operation, Andy. He started really evaluating his life and what he should do next. He was very much aware of his style but unwilling to take any risks to change. It was at this time that he hired me to coach him in finding a new career.

THE STRATEGIC TACTICIAN

Being that Andy was highly analytical he should have used it to his advantage in a strategic manner. Instead of letting fears drive him to a point of analysis paralysis, he should have used those skills as a strategic advantage and become The Strategic Tactician.

REACH OUT APPROACH IN ACTION

The analysis paralysis style severely hindered Andy's ability to maximize his and his team's potential. His risk-averse behavior robbed him of great satisfaction both professionally and personally. Instead, he could have become better able to come to powerful conclusions to his findings and then developed tactical plans to implement his strategies. To better connect, Andy could have done the following:

- Pass on his analytic skills to members of his team and allow them to make their own decisions.

- Become better at delegating – as a leader he was way too hands on.

- Learn to take good calculated risks – step out of the box a bit.

- Don't fear failure but let it be used as an opportunity to learn. With his high analytic skills, he could analyze not only from successes but also failure. His lack of learning from risk taking stunted his growth – both personally and professionally.

- Realize that one of his biggest downfalls is his risk aversion, which often led to him not making decisions and thus forcing him to suffer from analysis paralysis.

Now, if you are a Compliant Style are you a "analysis paralysis" type or "strategic tactician?"

This provides you with the basics on the High C, Compliant Style. To help you identify this style in action, think of people you interface with who represent this style.

Chapter 7 - Reach Out Approach Skill Builder Questions:

1. Do you think you have a High C communication style? If so, why do you think so?

2. Do you know anyone personally who exhibits High C communication style? If so, list them.

   - List what attributes make you think so.

   - Do you communicate and connect well with them?

     - If so, why?

     - If not, why?

3. List five public figures who exhibit High C communication style.

4. Upon review of the four communication styles, what is your style? High D, I, S or C?

   - Primary High Style

   - Secondary High Style

Chapter 7 Notes:

REACH OUT AND DEVELOP A CONNECTION BY READING STYLES

Now that you have a good understanding of the four behavior styles, you have a solid foundation to help you reach out and initiate communication with others. The next step is to develop a plan to connect by reading the styles of those people with whom you interact – even those difficult folks.

The first step in developing the connection with others is very simple: Put away your personal agenda and simply learn to understand others by reading them. As discussed in Chapter 3, we are all as unique as fingerprints and snowflakes. So get away from your needs and wants and build a sincere desire to understand others. Learn to understand them. Observe them. Listen to them, learn from and about them and put yourself in their shoes so to speak. As Stephen Covey said so many years ago in his excellent book *The Seven Habits of Highly Effective People*, "Seek first to understand then be understood." Or in other words, learn to walk in someone else's moccasins.

BE IN THE MOMENT!

Another phrase that resonates in this instance is "Be in the moment!" To develop a connection by reading others, you should have no other agenda than to understand them when you are with them.

Unfortunately, when we are interacting with others, most of us come from our point of view of the world. We are concerned about our agenda, our own needs. Now to be sure, this is completely natural so I am not being judgmental. In fact, I think it is natural. If you truly want to differentiate yourself as an effective communicator and ensure that you will connect with others you need to understand them first, temporarily putting what you desire on the back burner.

Remember that the Reach Out Approach is a people-centric approach.

Thinking of others first does not mean you subordinate your needs. You just put those needs temporarily on the back burner.

In fact, if you patiently follow this process it will help you attain those things you need and desire because you will see how they fit in with other's needs. But first, you need to understand them.

CLOSING THE COMMUNICATION GAP

You will also become better at connecting because you will close the communication gap. The communication gap represents the gap we have in connecting with someone else. That gap varies with all people we come into contact with. Some folks have issues with connecting more than others. The point is that there is most likely some sort of gap – large or small. By understanding others first, you take a vital step in closing that gap. Then naturally, when you make the approach to appeal to others by developing the connection with them, others will draw closer to you. This closes the gap even more and enables the opportunity to connect more. This helps ensure both parties secure what they need from a connection – a "win-win!" We are not seeking "utopian" communication, just closing the gap so we are significantly better at communicating than before.

I would see this process work, or not work, in the sales world all of the time. As a sales manager it would often amaze me, watching my sales reps interact with buyers. Oftentimes, the sales reps were so out of synch with what the buyer was saying and requesting. The reason? The sales rep was focused on his or her agenda and not the needs of the buyer. This situation ties back to the solution-selling model I mentioned in Chapter 1. By developing an understanding of your customers' needs and then seeing how your capabilities can solve their problems, ensures you meet the needs of your client. This helps the sales rep close the sale by becoming viewed as a partner and trusted business advisor rather than simply another vendor.

The Reach Out Approach I am speaking of is the same. Think of others first! Your needs will be fulfilled once you find the connection and effectively engage with someone. Just as the sales reps who applied the customer-centric solution selling model raised their value by becoming a trusted business advisor, so can you become as valuable and trusted to those with whom you reach out to every day. Once you've reached this level with people, you can in turn secure those things that your heart desires – success, prosperity and mastery as defined by you. You can accomplish this because you will be able to successfully work with and through people to achieve common goals. As stated throughout this book, the key to achieving any results you desire almost always involves working with others. The Reach Out Approach three-step process of initiate, develop and leverage provides you with the tactics to become a master at human interaction and communication.

YOU'RE ONLY HUMAN

Now, going back to the sales people I managed, they are only human and have many things on their minds so it is very easy to forget about the customers needs – they are trying to close the sale, chase quota, please their manager, deal with "fire drills" and their personal lives. What I'm saying is it's easy to subordinate or forget the needs of the customer. But this is also the most crucial mistake a sales rep can make! The customer comes first. Listen to them; understand their needs. This is what differentiates poor sales reps from good ones and great ones from good ones. The process of being an effective communicator and the art of connecting is exactly the same, quoting Covey again, "Seek first to understand then be understood." I would hit this point with my reps time after time because it is easy to get caught up in all that is going on versus truly listening to the customer.

DEVELOPING A CONNECTION
BY READING OTHERS

The art of developing a connection involves the ability to understand others by reading them. So now that you have a thorough understanding of the four base behavior styles in Chapters 4-7, let's learn to develop a connection by reading those behavior styles of the people you interact with.

When conducting workshops using the DISC behavioral assessment, I train participants to read the styles of others by using what I call Primary and Secondary Reads. Reads are basically cues, or behaviors to watch out for when interacting with others.

When I played football, each position on defense had "keys" or "reads." These were attributes we would focus on with the offensive player that would give us a clue as to what they would be doing on a given play. In high school and college I was a defensive back. My "key" or "read" was to watch the offensive tackles first. If they blocked "down" it indicated a running play and I would react accordingly to stop the run. My secondary read was then the quarterback to the running back to see who had the ball so I could tackle them.

If the offensive tackle pass blocked, I knew it was a pass play and would in turn go to my second read, the quarterback and then wide receiver to react accordingly to defend against the pass. These base "reads" were instilled in us every practice. They provided a foundation for us to successfully anticipate our opponent's offensive plays to stop them. The "reads" were very important, first knowing them and then applying them during practice in preparation for the game. You see, each player on a football team has their "reads." And the ability to "read" opponent's moves and plays accurately determines whether or not the team wins or loses. The "reads" are a fundamental element of football and used on every play of the game.

PRIMARY AND SECONDARY READS

In keeping with that same philosophy, there are foundational "reads" in identifying people's communication styles. I train on these "reads" in my workshops to help the participants learn to read the communication styles of those with whom they interact or connect – to identify if someone is a High D, I, S or C. I train on these reads using instructional videos. First, I train the participants on the "reads" and then we practice "reading" with the videos. The beauty of this process is that you can practice this skill every day on everyone you interface with. The reads are not rocket science. They are basic and easy. All it takes is your commitment to learn them; practice and you'll become a master at reading the behavior/communication styles of others.

In my workshops, I train on what I call **Primary and Secondary Reads.**

Primary Reads: The Primary Read is the first thing I want you to review when interacting with someone else. In using the behavior model for communication, the Primary Read involves identifying another person's Descriptors and Indicators from the DISC style profiles we discussed in Chapters 4 – 7.

> *Simply put, the Primary Read will help you identify the Primary Style as well as Secondary Style (not to be confused with Primary and Secondary Reads).*

As an example, if I am meeting someone for the first time I am going to determine what **Descriptors** best describe that person (are they aggressive, gregarious, relaxed, analytical and etc.). Then walk through the three **Indicators** we discussed for each style.

- Indicator #1: Is the person Extroverted or Introverted?

- Indicator #2: Is the person People-Oriented or Task-Oriented?

- Indicator #3: Is the person Direct or Indirect?

If I am speaking with someone who is outgoing, talkative and gregarious, I begin thinking this person is exhibiting High I behavior, because those words best describe a High I. As I continue observing, I walk through the three Indicators as well. Is the person Introverted or Extroverted? Is the person People-Oriented or Task-Oriented? Is the person Direct or Indirect? After observing and clarifying, I begin to get a decent profile of their communication style. I use both:

- **Common-Threads** – Looking for common attributes to validate my thought and

- **Process of Elimination** – To eliminate what is non-existent.

As I walk through this process I get a good gauge of their style and it gives me my first opportunity to develop a connection. Let's look at the following two examples:

- Tom is very forward, a go-getter, highly driven. He loves challenges and new projects. He is extroverted, task-oriented and direct. Based on this information, what behavior style is Tom?

- Kim is a great people person. She is not the life of the party, but excellent one on one. She is a steady performer, and has a methodical approach to solving problems. She is introverted, people-oriented and indirect. Based on this information, what is behavior style is Kim?

If you said, Tom was a High D and Kim was High S you are correct. Pretty easy, right? In that example, yes, as those were clear-cut examples. Unfortunately, it is not always so easy.

Keep in mind we are, indeed, all snowflakes and fingerprints and hence most people are blended styles as mentioned in Chapter 3. In fact, I play with this a bit in my workshops when after I review the styles I ask the class to determine the DISC behavior style of Bill and Hillary Clinton. This is a fairly easy read and most people guess Bill Clinton as a High I and Hillary as a High D, which is correct. Think about it, Bill Clinton is known for his gregarious, people-friendly persona. At a moment's notice, he'll bite his lower lip and "feel your pain." He has a way with people. Meanwhile Hillary Clinton, is known for her direct-ness and determined nature.

Then I ask folks do determine the behavior style of George W. Bush. In every class about half the room says High D, the other half says High I. Again, to some extent they are both correct as "W" is a blend of those two styles; I would say the Primary Style, whether it is High D or High I, is situational. He has his moments when he is very jovial and having fun with reporters or friends, but the other side is where he is quite forceful, direct, aggressive and decisive with some policy issues.

The point is you have easy "pure" style reads like Bill and Hillary Clinton and "blended" style reads like George W. Bush.

This drives home the message that our communication styles are a bit more complex than simply four styles. But the DISC behavioral tool provides us with a fairly quick way to read and connect with others. It also forces us to think out of the box and observe and listen to others.

I believe it is a selfless process that forces us to pay attention, listen and observe. It is people-centered.

Once the initial read is complete, then **Secondary Reads** take place.

Secondary Reads: The secondary reads I focus on is reading how people deal with change, risk and conflict. There are possibly other secondary reads you can use, but I find change, risk and conflict a good one. Reading these three areas may be difficult at first discussion, but once it is identified it gives a good validation to the primary read. By understanding how people deal with these three situations tells me a great deal about their styles and can validate my thoughts based on the primary reads.

Now to become proficient at developing a connection you must become a pro at questioning and listening. I am not just talking about asking mundane questions and vaguely listening. I am talking about questioning with a purpose and listening to hear and understand.

As an example, if I am struggling between someone being a High D or C, I can use the secondary read to validate my thoughts. If the person is a risk taker, loves change and is a "fighter" then I am going with the High D versus C. The change, risk and conflict factors are a bit more clear-cut. The only problem is how to identify in a discussion…well, by asking questions, listening and learning about the other person will, indeed, tell a great deal.

The reason I focus on the primary and secondary reads is that I want you to focus on something to help you read the styles – it is your foundation for reading styles to enable you to develop a connection. As you read in Chapters 4-7, there are several ways and words to help you understand the four styles. The process of primary and secondary reads helps you focus on simple, easy to read cues. Once you master the primary and secondary reads you can move to other verbiage to validate your thoughts.

EFFECTIVE QUESTIONING AND LISTENING SKILLS

The key to becoming effective at developing the connection by reading styles is to ask great questions and become a superb listener.

Questioning with a Purpose – Questioning with a purpose is an art form. The goal of questioning with a purpose is about asking questions to get the other person to talk, and provide you with information. This allows you to get to know and understand them. Unfortunately, I've found that most of us aren't very good at asking questions, at least not very good ones. I actually prove this theory in a workshop module I conduct called "The Name Game."

The Name Game is one of the most enjoyable modules I conduct in my workshops. Basically, the Name Game is like the game twenty questions. I go to the front of the room and portray someone in the news and based on questioning and listening skills the participants must try to guess who I am (A favorite I play to stump the participants is Condoleezza Rice. After all, who would think I would be portraying an African-American woman?). The rules entail that each person is only allowed to ask one question then they must go to the next person who asks another question. The purpose is to have each person build off of the prior question to in turn try and guess who I am as quickly as possible. What is so amazing to me about the times I play this game is how bad the questions are and how poor the listening skills.

What normally happens is that we go around the room, say of ten to fifteen folks at least twice and they haven't even come close to guessing who I am. The first mistake about ninety percent of the participants make is that they ask me solely "closed ended" questions that require a simple yes or no answer. A closed question is fine, when it is driving to gain closure but not for every question. The problem with it is that nothing gets resolved with solely closed ended questions. In this module, they didn't get me to open up or talk – in other words they didn't initiate or develop a connection to leverage a relationship with me – in other words, they didn't get me to open up and communicate with them. I just sit back and coyly respond to the closed ended question with a simple "yes, no, or maybe." Basically any one-word response I can give that provides little information about who I am. The point isn't to punish them, but to prove to them that they need to do much more to learn who I am and to get me to talk.

Now imagine what these folks are like when interacting with others. Most likely a mundane one-sided discussion, so imagine how monotonous this can be for the person who is being asked the questions. If it is a salesperson, this approach must drive a customer crazy. If it is a manager, this approach must drive an employee nuts. There is no way you will connect with this approach.

The second point is that most folks don't listen or build off the previous question, so little if any progress is made. Most folks are so caught up in their mindset and what they want to say that they don't listen much to the previous questions to make any correlations whatsoever.

The overarching goal of this session is to prove how poor our dialogue really is – how poor our question and listening skills – and, unfortunately, I always achieve my goal. You will never master the art of effective communication if you are a poor questioner and listener.

The key to success in this game as well as any one in which you are trying to learn about someone is to get them to open up and share so you can learn from them. The best way to do that is to use various questioning techniques.

To understand and build your skill sets on questions, I've listed four basic questioning techniques below. There are actually many more, but these represent the four basic ones. In addition, I listed when to use each:

- **Open Ended – A broad diagnostic question which encourages someone to talk**

- **Close Ended – Used to obtain a specific answer and to check facts**

- **Rhetorical – Used to summarize**

- **Probing – Used to probe a certain point or glean more information**

The key is to use these various questions at appropriate times in conjunction with each other to get the other person talking about themselves. The more you can do that the more you learn about them and the more you can connect and subsequently leverage the relationship for effective communication. So the point of improving your questioning skills is several-fold:

- To put your needs secondary

- To learn as much information about the other person so that you can determine their communication style

- To effectively connect

Listening Skills – The key to effectively listen is, well, LISTEN! You must listen to understand and to truly hear what someone is actually saying in addition to building a common-thread pattern to better understand someone else's point of view.

It is imperative to know that effective listening is a skill; it is the most energetic of the communication skills. It is the most effective way to understand other peoples needs and get the full benefit from your questioning skills, and the most important thing to remember about effective listening is:

You have two ears and one mouth!

GOOD VERSUS BAD LISTENING

To further understand the importance of listening, let's differentiate between effective and non-effective listening skills:

Effective Listening:

- Listen to understand not contradict

- Show by your manner that you are listening, i.e. active listening

- Assume what the other person is saying is important

- Take note of what is being said; do not ignore or disregard it

- Check your understanding by repeating back what you heard

- Listening is important to enable you to understand, retain and pass on the information

Ineffective Listening:

- Jumping to conclusions – where the listener fills in the blanks and draws incorrect conclusions

- Belief that others think like you – the belief that others have the same convictions

- The closed mind – the listener's refusal to hear things which contradict long held beliefs

- Selective listening – listening only when you feel the topic is relevant to you

- A lack of attention – most people think three to four times faster than they speak so sometimes their attention wanders

- Excessive talking – not giving someone else the opportunity to speak

The point of reviewing the art of effective questioning and listening is to enable you to become a master at reading styles. Your ability to read styles will be fundamentally important in building your skills at connecting which in turn enable you to effectively communicate.

Practice your skills - Listen & develop a meaningful connection by reading styles

Want more opportunities to practice the skills you learned in this chapter?

Go to the Reach Out Approach website, and listen to four 1-2 minute audio vignettes.

These brief vignettes will provide you with intriguing information about the important role Descriptors and Indicators play in *listening and reading* styles.

www.reachoutapproach.com/skillpractice

Chapter 8 - Reach Out Approach Skill Builder Questions:

1. You now know how to develop a connection by reading the styles of others. Go back to Chapter 3 and review the information you captured on the person you have "difficulty" communicating with. Using Primary and Secondary reads, identify this person's communication style. Are they High D, I, S, or C? What is this person's Primary High Style? Does this person exhibit a Secondary High Style?

   • Primary Reads –

      □ What words/descriptors did you capture and how do they match up against the four communication styles? As an example, if you listed "funny" could that be related to a High I. Conversely, could "tough" be related to a High D or maybe High C. Walk through this process with all of the words you listed and try to match each descriptor with one of the four communication styles.

      □ Did you list this person as more introverted or extroverted? Remember: D and I are extroverted while S and C are introverted.

      □ Did you list this person as more people-oriented or task-oriented? Remember: D and C are task-oriented while I and S are people-oriented.

□ Did you list this person as more direct or indirect? Remember: D and C are direct while I and S are indirect.

- What did you list regarding Secondary Reads?

  □ How does this person deal with change?

  □ How does this person deal with risk?

  □ How does this person deal with conflict?

2. Now using the process you learned in this chapter, determine the communication style of the "difficult" person. Remember to look for Common-Threads and use the Process of Elimination to narrow down this person's communication style.

- What is your "difficult" person's communication style? High D, I, S, or C?

  □ What is this person's Primary High Style?

  □ Do they have a Secondary High Style? If so, what is it?

3. Do you have the same communication style?

- What is the difference in your style versus this person?

- Where do "disconnects" exist?

Note: Capture this information thoroughly, as we will come back to this exercise in Chapter 9

Chapter 8 Notes:

REACH OUT AND LEVERAGE RELATIONSHIPS

Now that we've provided some tools to empower you to reach out by learning about four basic communication styles and develop a connection by learning how to read the styles of others when interacting with them, the next step is to leverage your style for effective communication – a mutually rewarding relationship. Now, exactly what do I mean by leverage?

Leveraging means wholly interacting with people to make a difference as well as a deep and lasting impression – to touch that emotional chord, whether it is in a relationship in your personal life or maybe a client relationship in your professional life. Remember my Tim Gard story? His subtle gesture was leveraged because it struck an emotional chord and made a long lasting impression – and had the all-important ripple effect I mentioned. His gesture touched me greatly but it also reached more than just me. Let me provide another strong example of someone leveraging a style with me – the story is actually about a customer who initiated a connection and made a powerful and lasting impression on me and my career.

THE REACH OUT APPROACH

LEVERAGING STYLES - A CUSTOMER WHO TAUGHT ME A VALUABLE LESSON

One of the toughest buyers in my twenty-five years of selling was head of procurement at F&M in Detroit. F&M was a deep discount retailer who sold mainly health and beauty aids but also some grocery products. I was twenty-four years old, wet behind the ears and was just promoted to key account manager. F&M was one of my customers and Joel was my buyer. Not only was Joel tough as nails, but he was also a seasoned veteran in his mid sixties so he had little tolerance for "young punks" like me trying to sell him things he didn't need or didn't sell. He was an off the charts high D style. In addition, he had a great deal of responsibility and pressure and had had a heart attack a year or so prior, so needless to say account calls with him were not a picnic. To make matters worse he was not only my largest account, he was one of the largest in our district and region. So nearly every month, my quota and that of the district and region hinged on what was sold to F&M… *and that oftentimes depended on the mood Joel was in that day.*

I had been calling on Joel for about four months when we were three months away from the close of the year. At that point my numbers at F&M were good, but calls with Joel had been nothing less than brutal. As much as I tried, I built little rapport with him. In fact, I didn't think he liked me very much at all. He simply tolerated me because he needed some of our products. I had not reached out or connected with Joel, let alone leveraged a relationship with him.

As I was preparing for an appointment with him, I was so excited because we were launching a new product and building a plan that Joel would "have to" like because we would sell a ton of product. There were other products like it so it was not a revolutionary product but, darn, I'm working hard for Joel here, and we'll sell a ton of it and I was sure of it.

So the day of my appointment, I showered and loaded on the Right Guard. You see, I needed a ton of deodorant because Joel liked to make me sweat. I owe losing about ten pounds to my calls with him – all ten lost IN THOSE CALLS – he was that intimidating. As I left my apartment, I felt confident that once and for all, I was going to show Joel how good of an account manager I was and how good this program was for his business. I would win him over and sell volumes upon volumes of OUR product.

So there I am, at F&M headquarters more confident than ever, when Joel walks out, doesn't say a word as usual and motions me to his office. To break the ice, I try some small talk, which Joel ignores as usual. He then asks me if I had anything "on deal" he needed to know about. At that moment, I started presenting OUR wonderful new product, how great OUR new product was and how much of OUR new product he would sell.

As usual Joel, emotionless, looked at me, looked straight at me and then did something strange. He stood up and walked towards the door, then told me to follow him outside. I was terrified thinking he was going to kick me out, call my boss – I had no idea what he was going to do. My Right Guard stopped working!

But he kept walking ahead of me and kept walking a few steps in front of me when he entered the store and walked towards the department of the new product I was attempting to sell him. You see F&M's corporate offices were located in one of their most profitable, and busy stores. I walked out and followed him.

At that moment, Joel did something amazing that I will never forget. He walked me to the department where my product was to be sold and took the time to explain to me about HIS business, about marketing, about HIS consumers, about growing HIS business, about satisfying HIS customers. He said I was too busy trying to sell MY product and not busy enough trying to grow HIS business and satisfy HIS customers. He let me know that OUR product was not revolutionary and did nothing to grow HIS business. In fact, my program would simply "rob Peter to pay Paul" as he liked to say, which meant that he would gain no new consumers, no incremental sales, would gain no category or store growth from our product. He said he would just sell more of MY product in lieu of one of my competitors, again "rob Peter to pay Paul." He said he could care less about our product, and most likely wouldn't even try it. He then gave me a lecture on how to build programs and promotions that would not only grow HIS business and not only make HIS customers happy but would in turn help ME sell more products.

At that time I realized I was getting a free course in Marketing 101, Customer Service 101 and Selling 101 via the school of hard knocks. I will say it was tough, but of more value than I can tell you. That difficult day with Joel did more for my career than I can tell you. It taught me to be a great salesman by thinking first about your customer's needs before your own, and by doing so you can build programs to not only meet their needs but yours as well. I was taught this in my training with the company I worked for, but it was so easy to forget, especially when "chasing a number" and getting enthused about your own brand. It was easy to forget about the customer, but also the one thing you should never forget.

This was 1987, and in a few minutes timeframe Joel taught me about category management and solution selling before they were even a thought in someone's mind and became hip in the 1990s.

In addition, Joel did something with me that this book is about – he reached out and connected. The lesson he taught me over twenty years ago still resonates. He reached out, communicated with me and taught me lessons whose repercussions have touched thousands, people I've sold to, managed, trained and spoken to over the years. That moment of initiating communication, developing the connection and leveraging the relationship was invaluable.

As we returned to his office, he did not buy our new product, and overall it was a bad call. I pleaded with him that his competition was buying it and again he reminded me that if it didn't grow his business, then he didn't care who had it.

I missed my sales quota for that month and caught some hell from my manager. But the next two months, I blew my number out of the water and closed the year well above quota. The reason why? Because all of my plans from then on with Joel and all my clients thereafter, were built around thinking about MY CUSTOMER FIRST! In addition, they were built around satisfying my customer's customer, the all-important consumer. They were built around growing THEIR category, not just MY brand. They were built around growing their CUSTOMER'S business and not just mine. And you know what? A funny thing happened. My business grew as well. It was a "win-win-win" for me, my customer and the consumer.

My selling skills were changed forever. My business knowledge was changed forever. My life was changed forever; all because a tough old buyer made the effort to reach out and connect with me. And truth be told, enabled me to effectively communicate with others as well, including you.

Now, as a next step, by learning to adapt styles you can effectively leverage your relationship with others. I am not speaking of changing who you are or acting deviously. I am speaking about appealing to someone else because you are appealing to how they communicate and connect. In the example of Joel, he was a tough guy, but he saw a way to teach me something valuable and knew I would learn better by taking me out to the store where the lesson would resonate with me more. He appealed and adapted to me which in turn enabled him to leverage his relationship with me. The ripple effect is still in play to this very day.

TO CONNECT OR DISCONNECT – THE PATHWAY TO LEVERAGING A RELATIONSHIP

Before Joel connected with me I was disconnecting with him – primarily because I didn't reach out and try to understand him, his business and his customers. The key reason many of us don't communicate well is because we have a disconnect and then cannot engage. Let me give you a few examples of how easily disconnects can manifest, just based on different behavior/communication styles.

Scenario #1: A sales rep, Alicia, is calling on a buyer, Zack. Their behavioral attributes are listed below:

- Buyer – Zack is direct, straightforward, forthright and fact based

- Sales Rep – Alicia is gabby, talkative, emotional, extroverted

    ▫ What is the DISC style of Zack? Alicia?

    ▫ Based on their style differences, what problems might exist, creating a disconnect?

Scenario #2: A personal relationship where their behavioral styles are listed below:

- Boyfriend - Sam is analytical, risk averse, quiet, numbers oriented

- Girlfriend - Tammy is direct, forward, aggressive,

    ▫ What is the DISC style of Sam? Tammy?

    ▫ Based in their style differences, what problems might exist, creating a disconnect?

Scenario #3

- Manager - Kim is friendly, introverted, methodical, relaxed

- Subordinate - Ralph is risk averse, analytical, direct, and careful

    ▫ What is the DISC style of Kim? Ralph?

    ▫ Based on their style differences, what problems might exist, creating a disconnect?

As you can see in the three scenarios it is simple to see how and where disconnects in communication might occur. Because the styles are different, there is a chance for a disconnect. Now, I am not saying that all differing styles have a disconnect, but most likely when a disconnect occurs it is because of differing styles.

THE OPPOSITE EFFECT – DISCONNECTING WITH ME

When I decided to build my speaking business, I became inundated with organizations who claimed they could help me build my business. They ranged from people saying they could help me "learn the ropes" of the speaking world to organizations that said they were speaking associations, not unlike the NSA, who could market me. I spoke with many of these companies and I was either unimpressed or disappointed at the little results they provided. The bottom-line was none of them made the connection or leveraged the relationship with me.

One organization was relentless and kept calling and emailing me. The company claimed they had the resources to help me market my business, get me in front of key meeting planners and land me speaking gigs. I was skeptical because of my previous unsatisfying experiences. I explained my disappointment with the woman who contacted me and she said she understood and heard of this from other clients. She then promised me that I would not be disappointed and that she would take personal responsibility for my account. Before I decided to work with them we had several calls that went this same route. My purpose was really to test her commitment. She seemed authentic, gave me a reasonable price to work with them, so I decided to move forward – big mistake!

Now, a week after I paid them and provided them with some of my marketing collateral so they could help market me, she missed three phone appointments to discuss our plan of action for my business. After each missed call she would call or email me a few days later to apologize. After the fourth call, I had enough and asked for my money back. After clearly discussing my apprehension in the first place it was unconscionable that she would miss one call let alone four. She clearly didn't read me or she would have connected with me. She had now lost me.

At that time her boss got involved and said they would not refund my deposit. She apologized and said she would handle my account from now on, and no problems would occur. I reluctantly agreed and we scheduled a conference call two days later. She assured me I would get the customer service I deserved and as expected – she missed the call! This made for five missed conference calls in a span of two and a half weeks. Needless to say, I stopped working with them. In addition, I mention my experience with this organization to anyone I can, hoping I can save them from wasting their money like I did with them. As I found out later, this company had a terrible reputation in the speaking industry.

The moral of this story is that top-notch customer service organizations apply the Reach Out Approach of initiating, developing and leveraging relationships with their customers – they communicate effectively. If they don't they lose the business. This company not only lost me but when I tell people about how bad an organization they are and how bad my experience was, well, a negative ripple effect has taken place. Just as a positive ripple effect takes a natural positive motion a negative ripple effect takes a negative motion. If you are in the customer service business, service your customer – reach out and connect with them and the ripple effect will pay tenfold in the positive.

As shown in these examples it is easy to see where problems and disconnects can arise. It doesn't matter if it is a professional or personal environment, these type of disconnects occur every day. The point is for us to realize where disconnects can occur and in turn connect so we can leverage the relationship for effective communication.

Now the process of leveraging the relationship is simple – Just adapt your style to be more like the person you are interacting with. And I don't mean to change who you are, but realize where they are coming from and how they are communicating and be more accommodating of that style.

LEVERAGING THE 4 COMMUNICATION STYLES

LEVERAGING COMMUNICATION WITH A HIGH D:

One of my toughest clients, Bart, was a high-level vice president in a large company. I was brought in to coach him as he had some issues in his managerial approach. Although he was a very nice and friendly guy he was also very confident and opinionated. He had a lot of issues with both his direct team and his colleagues. They found him very hard to work with and he was "gumming up the works" on a new initiative the company was launching. When it came time to share information, he was possessive. When it came time to hear other opinions he was critical. And when it came time to make changes required with the initiative, he was obstinate. His approach to nearly everything was "my way or the highway," with colleagues and his team. Fortunately, he had little if any interface with external clients, but his internal clients in the company struggled with him. He was really causing major issues not only to his team and colleagues, but to the company as a whole.

So the company brought me in to work with him. In working with him he was the High D behavior style and it was easily noticeable. Although he gave the impression to embrace the coaching process, he did nothing to progress in his development. This went on for several months. Basically, he was being accommodating because the company mandated he be coached.

After a few months, I'd tried several approaches to get him to move forward and none of which seemed to resonate for long periods. Finally, it all came to a head when he had a major blowout with several colleagues in a meeting. It got so ugly that even he knew he was in trouble.

Realizing I had not yet connected with him, I came up with an idea almost on the spot in our next coaching session. In our discussion, I asked him if he liked boxing to which he replied that he did enjoy it. At that point I used boxing as a metaphor to describe him and his behavior. I asked him, in his opinion what type of boxer is known to be better, a "slugger" or someone who could "stick and jab." He said someone who could "stick and jab." Then I asked why. He said, sluggers merely punch for the sake of punching and normally wear themselves out. He admired the "stick and jab" fighters for their patience and knowing when to throw a punch and when not to. They knew when to pull back and when to unload. He described them as strategic while a slugger was not at all. We basically went through several examples of the differences when suddenly I asked him, "In this work environment and especially the recent blow up situation, which boxer type would you describe yourself as?"

At that point it hit him like a ton of bricks. Initially he said "strategic," but the evidence of his behavior was too strong so he capitulated and said "slugger." At that point, I connected with him. It was then that he totally opened up and we had a very strong and meaningful discussion about his behavior with his team and colleagues. That simple yet powerful metaphor opened his eyes and resonated with him. This tough nut who I was struggling to connect with was now quite aware of his poor behavior. That he was acting like a "slugger" and a poor one at that. We now had a very powerful connection, which allowed me to effectively coach him. That was not the only time I used a metaphor with him. In fact, whenever I wanted to make a strong point I used one and it worked like a charm. I realized that was the way to help educate and to get him to look inward and see areas he needed to work on.

The bottom-line, this was a High D style and my approach to connect and communicate was exactly like they respond. The metaphors I used were direct, to the point, fact based and hence they resonated with him. This is how you approach a High D behavior style. I'm not saying a metaphor is the only way to go, but in this instance the simplicity, directness and hard-hitting point really resonated with him. That is the key with this style. If you can win them over and connect you have won the battle.

So here are some simple clues as to how you can leverage your style based on the DISC communication styles:

When interacting with the High D Style – The key to leveraging communication with a High D is to get to the point with accurate, fact based data and be direct.

**Things to do when communicating with a High D –
Communication Do's**

- Be clear specific and to the point

- Stick to business

- Provide facts and figures for success

- Be prepared with support material, objectives

- Provide alternative solutions[22]

**Things not to do when communicating with a High D –
Communication Don'ts**

- Don't talk about things not relevant to the issue

- Don't leave loopholes of cloudy issues

- Don't appear disorganized[23]

Keys to motivating a High D

- Allow them to control their destiny

- Give them power and authority

- Provide them with prestige, position and titles

- Allow opportunity for advancement

- Assist them in pacing themselves[24]

Keys to managing a High D

- Clearly explain expected results

- Negotiate commitments one-on-one

- Define rules

- Confront disagreements face-to-face

- Assist them in pacing themselves[25]

These points illustrate how to engage with a High D, let's move on to the High I whose method of leveraging communication style is quite different.

LEVERAGING COMMUNICATION WITH A HIGH I:

My client, Sue, was in an accounting role. She was excellent in her job and was promoted into a role as a manager. This was the first time she ever managed people. The company brought me in to help transition her in the role. She had been in the job for about six months and was struggling, specifically with the people-side of the new role.

When I started with her she was working well with most of her team of six, with one exception, Jim. Sue and Jim were like oil and water, diametrically opposite people. Sue was an extremely High C. She was analytical, reserved, quiet, introverted and risk averse. To help her understand Jim, we profiled his behavior style. As it turned out Jim was very High I, he was extroverted, talkative, outgoing, gregarious and emotional – again, the total opposite of Sue. Sue was having a great deal of trouble connecting with Jim. In addition, Jim was not performing well and had some issues with clients.

As part of the team's development, Sue had weekly one-hour meetings with each of her team members individually. She wanted to use our coaching work to focus on helping her use the hourly meetings with Jim as an opportunity to develop him. Prior to our work, the time Sue spent with Jim was monotonous for her. During that hour, Sue couldn't seem to focus Jim for long. In fact, every time they started getting work accomplished Jim would drift off into some tangent and away from the task at hand. Being a High C, this drove Sue bonkers plus they didn't end up accomplishing the task at hand.

As we worked the profile on Jim, I worked with Sue to identify how she, a High C could connect with Jim a High I, very opposite styles. When we talked about connecting, Sue realized that in order to connect with Jim she would indeed need to engage his I-style more - To begin a dialogue with Jim and to engage in discussion; in other words, be more like a High I.

A few weeks went by where I didn't push Sue on the issue as we worked on other areas of her development. I wanted to let her take the initiative to try to connect. One day Sue mentioned to me how the relationship between she and Jim had improved. When I asked what transpired, she said that during the last few hourly meetings with Jim, she spent the first five to seven minutes socializing with him. She made small talk, asked Jim about his weekend and basically spent time getting to know him. When I asked how it went, she laughed and said the first five to seven minutes were very tough for her. Being the High C she just didn't want to socialize at all but wanted to dive into the task at hand. But she said a strange thing happened now that she spent the upfront time socializing. After those few minutes, the remainder of the time spent with Jim was highly productive. Jim seemed content that she had shown interest in his personal life and was then ready to work. Sue said it was well worth it as they now had very productive sessions and also, improved relations with the client. Overall, Jim's performance improved as well.

Sue had successfully leveraged this relationship. It ultimately made life better for her, Jim and the client. It was a win-win-win for everyone. Again the positive ripple effect of reaching out, communicating and connecting came to fruition once again.

This is common when leveraging styles with High I's. In fact, I liken it to when I worked as an area manager many years ago. At the time, I managed a team of thirteen sales folks in the entire state of Florida. Our team included four Hispanic reps in the Miami marketplace. The days I spent working with them in Miami were some of the fondest. I can speak decent Spanish but I am not fluent. However, when I went into account calls with my reps, I attempted to speak Spanish and both my reps and customers appreciated it. They spoke English and most of the call was done in English as well, but the point is that they were pleased that I tried. In addition, whenever I was offered a shot of Cuban coffee in a customer call, I gladly obliged. Again, they were pleased that I did and it helped build the rapport. Now, after a day of doing about eight Cuban coffees I was ready to jump out of my skin, but it was all worth it as it helped build rapport and our business prospered. Simply put, I immersed myself in their culture. I understood them. In general, Hispanics are very sociable and like to socialize as it helps build trust. Now I am not saying all Hispanics are High I style, but again their culture is one whose emphasis is on building rapport and trust. Hence,

I did what I could to accommodate and for this reason reach out and connect.

When interacting with the High I Style – The key to leveraging communication with a High I is to be as personable, open and friendly as possible. It is imperative to build rapport, a relationship.

Things to do when communicating with a High I – Communication Do's

- Talk about people and their goals

- Ask for their opinion

- Allow time for relating and socializing

- Focus on people and action items

- Be stimulating fast and fun[26]

Things not to do when communicating with a High I – Communication Don'ts

- Don't be cold, curt

- Don't control the conversation

- Don't drive in facts and figures or abstractions[27]

Keys to motivating a High I

- Environment free from control and data

- Popularity and social recognition

- Freedom of speech and people to talk to

- Identification with a team

- Public recognition for their ability[28]

Keys to managing a High I

- Assist in setting realistic goals

- Develop friendship with daily interaction

- Allow freedom of movement, no control

- Open door policy to discuss issues

- Set in jobs with people interaction[29]

LEVERAGING COMMUNICATION WITH THE HIGH S

My passion as a child was football. I ate, drank and slept it! Unfortunately, I was a little guy. In seventh grade I only weighed seventy-five pounds. But I was determined to play football, not only in high school but at the collegiate level as well. In fact, it was at that time that I focused my life, my vision and my goals on gaining size and strength to play football. I worked very hard. I spent what seemed like endless days and nights lifting weights with my friends, attaining goal after goal. I did everything – drinking protein shakes, eating raw eggs like Sylvester Stallone in the movie *Rocky*. I focused my whole life around the goal of playing high school and college football.

Through my hard work, I ended up becoming a very good high school football player. By my senior year, I was a 5'9, 170 All-Conference selection who helped lead the team to the play-offs. In fact I became so good I was recruited to play college football, and chose Allegheny College.

You see, a lot of my success in football came from friends and especially coaches who reached out, connected and communicated with me. They saw the hard work, knew my abilities and knew the size of my heart. I owe a great deal of that success to several friends and coaches who connected.

In addition, based on my High S style their ability to connect with me depended greatly on their approach. Even back then, I exhibited High S style behavior. I was very methodical, steady and deliberate in my approach to things. I wasn't a "rah-rah" type of guy nor was I "first out of the gate" on new ideas and new things. In addition, I didn't easily take advice at face value. I tended to listen and then move at the pace where I felt comfortable. This also meant that I did not respond well to "in your face" type coaching. I appreciated a patient conversational approach.

My favorite coaches knew how to reach me by building a one-on-one connection; they had faith in me and, most importantly, were patient with me. Because of my size, my development was slower but they saw the potential and nurtured it. Despite my size they showed confidence in me even when I made mistakes. They knew how to communicate with me. They didn't yell and scream and most often spoke with me in a patient conversational tone and, oftentimes, one-on-one carefully encouraging me, slowly building my confidence in them and their approaches. My favorite coaches engaged me because they appealed to my High S style.

When I went to play at Allegheny it was a different story. The head coach was older, very aloof and not a good communicator – basically he couldn't connect. His style of motivation ranged from the bizarre to the mysterious. In addition, he was distant and not easily approach-able. His efforts in reaching out were one-dimensional thinking each of the player's motivational and communication styles were the same. He would approach you and tell a story, a parable and expect you to learn a lesson from it. Now at my current age I might know what the lesson was and appreciate it. But at the time, as a twenty year old, my team-mates and I just didn't get it. I just wanted a coach I could connect with and who could communicate well. He would have done much better speaking his mind. Simply put, his approach did nothing for me. Now, some did respond to it and he was able to connect with them, but with a vast majority he did not do so well. In fact, his approach became a joke to most.

Because of his approach, football took on a new meaning for me. It lost some of its zest. I had a decent career, and made the All Century Team. But the experience was not as fun as it had been and our team suffered because of it with three consecutive losing seasons before the coach was let go.

The point of this story is once again, connection. Those who connect versus those who did not made a difference. Now to be sure, I am ultimately in charge of MY motivation. I don't want to sound like I was not in control of that aspect. In fact, it was most definitely my own motivation that enabled me to play in the first place and in college. However, when I was surrounded with coaches who could appeal to my High S style to connect it made the experience that much more rewarding. The ability to connect runs the gamut, from relationships, to leaders, to sales reps to football coaches. If you can find a way to connect you will have exponential success.

When interacting with the High S Style – The key to leveraging communication with a High S is to be patient, persistent yet not overbearing. Let them move at their own pace.

Things to do when communicating with a High S – Communication Do's

- Begin with personal comments, break the ice

- Show sincere and honest interest

- Move casually, informally

- Don't force decisions on them

- Present your case logically and non-threatening[30]

Things not to do when communicating with a High S – Communication Don'ts

- Don't rush headlong into business

- Don't be domineering or demanding

- Don't force them to respond quickly to decisions[31]

Keys to motivating a High S

- Logical reasons to change

- Harmony

- Closure on tasks

- Time to adjust to change

- Recognition for a job well done[32]

Keys to managing a High S

- Clearly explain changes to prepare them

- Encourage their contribution in meetings

- Involve them in long-term planning

- Assign them fewer, larger projects

- Allow opportunity to finish tasks started[33]

LEVERAGING COMMUNICATION WITH HIGH C

My client, Marcy, was a quiet, reserved and cautious woman with a passion for self-development. She hired me to coach her to become better at sales, especially around her need to conduct cold calling sales she did over the phone. Marcy was a High C style, very analytical, not quick to change and take risks. In addition, she was from South America so she was still having some cultural and language barriers that made her "walk on eggshells" a bit. My approach with her, my way of connecting was more about moving slowly but persuasively by using various factual and proven methods that let her take incremental risks and make changes at her own pace.

The method I used to connect with her was to help her learn about the four DISC behavioral styles and then teach her to profile the styles of her potential clients. We practiced leveraging the different styles for several weeks until she became quite proficient at it. As always, when comfortable, Marcy wanted to take it to the next level of practice, so she inquired how we might approach it. I recommended a series of role-play sessions where I would portray a client, and a specific behavior style and through questioning and listening skills she would determine my behavior/communication style and adapt/connect to close the sale.

We started these role-plays in person and face-to-face, then the next step we did it back to back, the purpose here was for her to improve her listening without seeing me. Then, once she became proficient, we did the role-plays via the phone, and so she could not see me, just hear me. She would call me and we would start the role-play immediately. I would answer as a client with a specific behavior style and based on the questioning and listening skills she would try to identify my style and then connect and communicate.

We did this for several weeks to the point where Marcy became excellent at it. The point is that I used an approach to connect with her based on her style to help her connect with her clients based on their styles. Basically, the approach I took helped her be more comfortable. My approach with her helped minimize the risk of trying a new method with cold call clients and it worked like magic.

When interacting with the High C Style – The key to leveraging communication with a High C is to be cautious, patient and very fact oriented.

Things to do when communicating with a High C – Communication Do's

- Prepare your case in advance

- Approach in a direct and straightforward way

- Present specifics and facts

- Take your time and be persistent

- Do not appeal to feelings[34]

Things not to do when communicating with a High C – Communication Don'ts

- Don't be giddy casual or informal

- Don't push too hard or be unrealistic with deadlines

- Don't be disorganized or messy[35]

Keys to motivating a High C

- No sudden or abrupt changes

- Time to think and analyze

- Reassurance that job is being done right

- Strong operating procedures in writing

- Objective tough problems to sell[36]

Keys to managing a High C

- Train them in people skills

- Encourage their contribution

- Involve them in defining standards

- Set attainable goals

- Clearly identify job expectations[37]

These above hints provide you with the roadmap you will need to successfully leverage communication style with others. Now to be sure, this is just the starting point, but they will eventually lead you to a deeper relationship with others by closing the communication gap.

STYLE INTERACTIONS

Lastly, keep in mind my comment earlier in this chapter that because styles differ doesn't automatically mean that they clash or there is a huge gap in communication, but most gaps in communication occur when styles differ. This is common sense. The general rule of thumb is that like styles tend to communicate and connect better. In other words, the chances are the communication gaps are smaller. There is one interaction in like styles when there could still be a bit of a gap. Any idea? Take a guess…

- A, D to a D?

- An, I to an I?

- An, S to an S?

- A, C to a C?

If you guessed, the D to the D, you are correct. Since these styles are so aggressive, direct and challenging – not to mention their conflict response is to "fight" – they are the most like styles that are most likely to clash.

Now, you have seen many examples throughout this book where communication style disconnects have caused clashes. We will now explore these interactions in depth in the next two chapters. Chapter 10 will review The Three Levels of Communication. Then in Chapter 11 we will see some real world situations of how the styles interact – to connect and communicate.

Reach Out Skill Practice

Practice your skills - Listen & leverage relationships by adapting styles

Would you like practice the skills you learned in this chapter?

Visit the Reach Out Approach website and listen to four brief 1 minute audio vignettes.

These interesting vignettes give you an opportunity to learn how to *adapt* your style so you can communicate more effectively.

www.reachoutapproach.com/skillpractice

Chapter 9 - Reach Out Approach Skill Builder Questions:

1. Now that you identified your communication style and that of your "difficult" person, use the tools you learned in this chapter to develop a plan of action to leverage communication with them?

   • What is your communication plan of action?

     ▫ What are your Do's in communicating with this person? List five things you'll now do when you communicate with this person.

     ▫ What are your Don'ts in communicating with this person? List three things you won't do when communicating with this person.

     ▫ If applicable, how will you motivate this person?

     ▫ If applicable, how will you manage this person?

2. Now that you have your communication plan of action, when will you reach out to this person?

   • Set a date

- List your results

- List what you need to do to continue improving your communication with this person

Chapter 9 Notes:

CHAPTER 10

MASTERING COMMUNICATION
INTERACTIONS

Y ou have now had a comprehensive overview of the three
steps of the Reach Out Approach: initiating, developing
and leveraging. This process will provide you with the skill
sets to not only become an effective communicator but to
differentiate yourself from others. This ability to differentiate will lead
you to results you desire; whether it be richer relationships, making
more sales, being an effective leader or being a better parent. The key is
you will now be able to make a difference when communicating with
others and have long lasting effects. Now, why do I mention differen-
tiation and why is it important?

In the world of marketing, a key to any brand success is to differentiate
itself from its competition. In addition, to illustrate the differences in
the features, attributes and added benefits the brand provides to the
end user, the consumer.

ARE YOU JUST ANOTHER BRAND OF
TOOTHPASTE, WHY SHOULD I BUY YOU?

In the branding world of toothpaste, it's often difficult for a brand to
differentiate itself because there are no innovations that one company

can make that another cannot in turn make. I am sure you've seen it; tartar control, plaque removal, all-in-one, sensitive teeth, etc. Basically, all toothpaste manufacturers have a product line to meet these consumer needs. In addition, there is not much difference in the way you can price or promote toothpaste – there just is not much wiggle room. Companies, regardless of what product they are selling, must differentiate themselves for success. That is a marketer's job.

Now, there are some great people and companies who "get it" and differentiate themselves very well. Two of my favorites are the Walt Disney World Resorts and Harley Davidson.

Walt Disney knew how to connect with the consumer. Regardless of how many times I've been to Epcot or any Disney Park, it is a magical experience. That is essentially the word everyone uses to describe their stay at any of the Disney locations – magical. What makes this amazing is that the Disney people are able to create these memorable experiences for families 365 days a year – and they do it year after year. That ability to create a nearly constant magical experience is what differentiates Disney from most other parks. After all, how many people could continue going to the same park and still have it seem like the first time? Walt Disney knew how to use the Reach Out Approach with the consumer and the ripple effect is outstanding – tons of wonderful experiences for millions of families across the globe.

Harley Davidson also does a great job differentiating itself from their competition. If I may ask you, "What does Harley Davidson sell?" If you said "motorcycles" you are, well, correct, in a way. In the book *Re-Imagine* by Tom Peters, he quotes a Harley Davidson executive on what they sell:

> *"What we sell is the opportunity for forty-three-year-old male accountants to dress up in leather, drive through small towns and scare people."*

In other words, they don't sell motorcycles; they sell the vision of excitement, risk and living on the edge for people who might not have it otherwise. They definitely differentiate themselves by initiating, developing and leveraging a connection with their consumer. Now, what do these two points have to do with this book?

> *The skills of initiating, developing and leveraging can differentiate you to achieve the success, prosperity and mastery you desire – personally and professionally!*

DIFFERENTIATE YOURSELF THROUGH EFFECTIVE COMMUNICATION

From a metaphor perspective, I often look at people's communication skills as "toothpaste," meaning it is rare to find people who differentiate themselves by making true connections. Think about some of the folks you've already read about in this book who differentiated themselves with me: Tim Gard, Joel, my buyer at F&M. In addition, there are folks like Coach Lombardi, Alvarez and Dick Winters, whom I don't know personally but who had a great influence that had positive ripple effects.

The beauty of the Reach Out Approach is it provides people who use it with a way of differentiating themselves and, in turn, greatly opens the door to help them succeed regardless of their endeavors. How many people do you know who consistently connect to positively affect the lives of others? With regard to people I interact with on a daily basis

I can count them on my hand – and possibly have fingers left over. Again, I am talking about consistently making connections where the ripple effects touch many others.

ONE-ON-ONE COMMUNICATION AND BEYOND

The key to the Reach Out Approach process is to improve communication – connection. So far we have mainly discussed the one-on-one aspect to effective communication. But the important thing to realize about this process is it reaches beyond just a one-on-one interaction. Oftentimes we need to communicate beyond an initial face-to-face interaction. As an example, it may be when a sales rep needs a buyer to sell an idea to higher-level folks in the organization, maybe someone in the C-Suite. It is imperative that the sales rep connects with the buyer so they will, in turn, connect with the person in the C-Suite. The one-on-one connection between the sales rep and buyer is important but it takes on an additional level of importance when the buyer needs to connect with their managers above them.

The process you're learning will improve your skills on a one-on-one level but also in a more advanced capacity as well. There are oftentimes when communication and connection scenarios become even more complex – to a multi-level connection. By mastering the one-on-one dynamic you will greatly improve your communication skills, but when you can master multi-level communication you will have truly differentiated yourself as a highly effective communicator. This is where you can raise the bar in your communication style, which enables you to not be just another tube of toothpaste, but to effectively communicate with others and have the ripple effects of a Walt Disney.

This chapter will help you first understand three types of communication interaction as well as provide you a game plan on how to specifically address all three in respective to your world.

THE THREE LEVELS OF COMMUNICATION

Basically, there are three levels of communication that I train my clients to learn about and master: Level 1, 2 and Multi-Level Communication.

Level 1 Communication – Level 1 represents a one-on-one communication interaction; primarily what has been discussed in this book so far. It consists of one person connecting and communicating with another person based on their behavior style. How do you interact with that person one to one and what do you need to do to connect with him or her based on their communication style?

In the following example, how does the Tom, a High D Style, communicate and connect with Geri, a High I? Well, based on what you learned in Chapter 9, you have your answer. Tom needs to be less forceful, aggressive and task-oriented and become more friendly, approachable and people-oriented. This example illustrates the basic Level 1 interaction between two people.

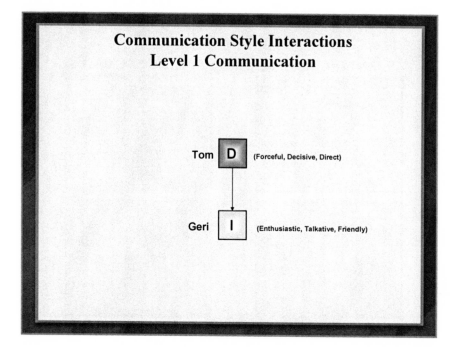

The key to Level 1 Communication is that each style must know how to connect with each of the other four styles as the following graph illustrates. To be effective the D person needs to learn to communicate/ connect with each of the other styles (I, S, C), including the D to D. And the same holds true for the other styles in terms of their need to learn to interact and connect with all four styles.

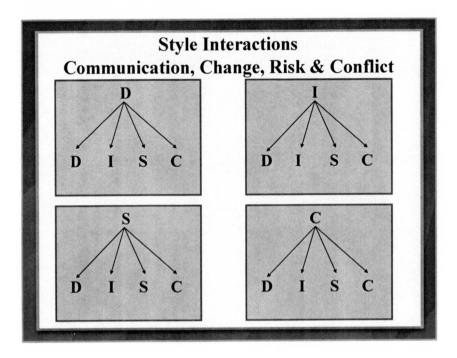

By learning the skill of effective communication through a connection, you can better gain great benefits in several areas of your life, both personally and professionally. Listed below are a few areas where you can benefit:

Level 1 Communication – Areas of Benefit:

- One-on-One Personal Relationships

  ▫ Marriage

  ▫ Friendships

  ▫ Personal relationship

  ▫ Parent to child

      □ Family member to family member

- One-on-One Professional Relationships

      □ Managerial – manager to employee

      □ Teammate to teammate

      □ Sales rep to customer

      □ Account manager to client

      □ Customer service to customer

Level 2 Communication – This level takes on a bit of complexity because it works by getting you to encourage another person to interact with a third person. An example would be a manager working with a subordinate calling on a client. The manager must connect with the subordinate first to in turn get them to connect with the third person, in this instance the client. This is typical in a managerial relationship, I call it "going to bat approach." How do I communicate to you to, in turn, help you better connect with someone else?

This skill is imperative for someone managing or leading others. In the following graphic you can see where Tom must effectively communicate with Jim so he can connect with Geri. In this example Tom is a High D and Jim is a High C. Tom needs to adapt to Jim in order to help him connect with Geri who is a High I. This is very common in the workplace and most often the reason communication breaks down – the styles are clashing. Plus, something almost always gets lost as styles pass on information to others who in turn must communicate it with someone else.

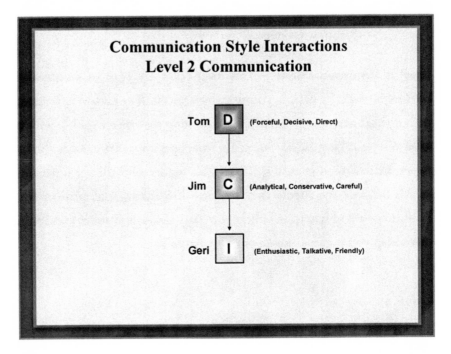

With the process you are learning in this book, you should become much better at the Level 1 Communication as well as Level 2. However, the key is to build your skills at the Level 1 arena. These skills are like building blocks so it is imperative you master the initial interaction first and foremost as it will build on the next level.

Like the previously mentioned example, this skill is also very useful for those relying on someone else to deliver a message to yet another. Level 2 Communication is also typical in a sales rep role when the key decision maker is not the direct buyer; it is someone higher on the totem pole (i.e. C-Suite). The sales rep must "sell the idea" or "connect" enough with the direct buyer so the direct buyer can in turn sell the idea to the higher level. This is again another example of "going to bat", meaning you are relying on someone else to "go to bat" for you, so you must ensure a strong connection so the message transfers seamlessly to the second person who seamlessly translates to the third person. The stronger this connection the more likely success is to occur.

CROSSING T'S AND DOTTING I'S

I learned a valuable lesson on the art of interactions and connection with a coaching client I had several years back. I was approached to work with Matt who was a manager at one of my clients. I met with Matt after running the DISC behavioral assessment on him. He was a High C style so he was quiet and reserved, and I must say not a risk taker and quite averse to change. When we worked on setting objectives for our training, his manager, Jean, wanted to be part of the process. This was fine by me as that is how I normally work. If the manager doesn't have input the coaching may lose some effect. The caveat was that Jean didn't feel she needed to meet me, but would walk through the objectives of the coaching with Matt who in turn would share with me. Then he and I would tweak and return to Jean for final approval.

From my discussions with Matt, I assessed that his manager Jean was a High D behavior style. We received the objectives and they seemed in line for me so we began the coaching process. As I said, Matt was very risk averse and oftentimes hesitant to make changes. So although some of his development was slow, I thought for an off the chart High C, he was making good progress. That was until the mid-coaching review with Jean. When Matt met with Jean to discuss his progress and results she became livid. Jean felt we accomplished nothing and that the coaching was a waste of time. She even threatened to cancel the session.

When I spoke with Matt in depth about this, the real problem hit me. I didn't help to effectively communicate with Jean. By meeting with her directly, which would have helped me reach out, connect and communicate with her I could have helped build expectations around the process and objectives we agreed upon. In other words, I could have better managed expectations with Jean.

You see, Jean was a High D; she is aggressive, fast-paced and results oriented. In addition, she was a big risk taker and loved change. Matt was the opposite. I made the mistake of not reaching out to Jean to set expectations on Matt's development and progress in coaching. It would be very hard to meet Jean's high expectations with Matt's slower cautious ways. Now, I think I moved Matt significantly faster than he thought or ever would have alone, he made great strides, but not in the eyes of Jean who had greater expectations. It was a lesson learned by me to set expectations for both the coachee and manager based on DISC behavior style, reaching out, developing the connection and leveraging before the process even began – lesson learned!

I was able to meet with Matt and discuss the dynamics, it cooled the situation and we continued the coaching, but some damage had been done and valuable time lost. Again, a lesson learned. I needed to use the Reach Out Approach with multiple people in this instance – both

Matt and Jean. This would have allowed me to manage the process and expectations better and ensure the coaching process was successful.

Listed below are a few areas where Level 2 Communication proves beneficial:

Level 2 Communication – Areas of Benefit:

- One-on-One Personal Relationships

  - Parental

  - Relationship

  - Family

- One-on-One Professional Relationships

  - Managerial to employee to client

  - Sales rep to customer to higher level contact

  - Account manager to client to higher level contact

  - Customer service to customer

Multi-Level Communication – This level entails dealing with multiple connection points in a group, possibly a team dynamic. This means understanding the unique communication dynamics of a team and having the flexibility to connect to the various dynamics on that team, individually and as a whole. This speaks to the quotes from Vince Lombardi, Barry Alvarez and Dick Winters I mentioned in Chapter 1 on how to push the buttons of the various folks on a team. You have to know not only how everyone communicates, but also how they each deal with change, risk and conflict as well. This ability to look at and connect with the team based on their unique style makeup is a true differentiating point of a successful manager or leader.

You can get a good gauge as to specific team dynamics as well. Are they risk takers? Are they change agents? Are they gregarious, quiet, analytical or aggressive? Or are they possibly a balanced blend? When I work with my clients on Multi-Level Communication, I call this their "team chessboard." By understanding the team dynamics, the chessboard, so to speak, managers can make better decisions on how to interact, connect and flesh out responsibilities. It also provides managers with a snapshot of potential strengths and weaknesses. A prime example of this was when a manager learns the respective communication styles of his staff – not only can he become more effective in communicating with them, but he can also develop an action plan for fleshing out responsibilities and giving them leadership roles based on the strengths of their style. You'll see yet another example of Multi-Level Communication in the next chapter but to glean some insights into this type of connection look at the following graphic.

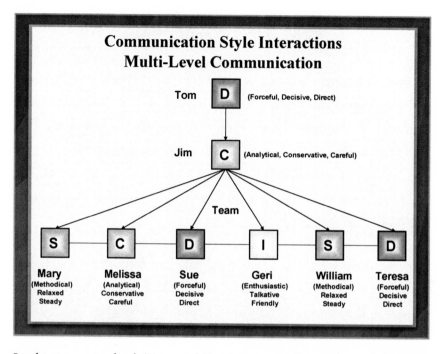

In this instance, both Tom and Jim have a good snapshot of the team dynamics. In fact, this scenario illustrates connection/interaction at all three levels. In this situation, Tom and Jim have a lay of the land of Jim's team. Most likely Tom has several other direct reports like Jim so this gives him an overview of just one of them. This example, however, represents Jim's "chessboard." As you can see Jim being a High C has each of the styles represented on his team. In fact, his team is a fairly balanced mix of all four styles. So to be effective Jim needs to learn to connect with each team member based on their styles. In addition, if he is really good, he'll pass on the skills set of reaching out, connecting and leveraging to his team so they function well together and with whomever else they interface with on a daily basis.

A LEADER STEPPING OUT OF THE BOX AND CONNECTING

As another example of how I've connected with a High D style, I used a similar approach. Randy was in a very high-level leadership position with a company in New York. Although he was not as tough as Bart from the previous chapter, he was a very confident man who held a great deal of responsibility and had a lot of people under him in his department. To make matters even more difficult, it was a highly political environment.

Now, working with Randy was quite different from Bart. Randy was a High D style, but he was very open to coaching and learning new things. In fact, he embraced most everything we worked on together. I connected with him early in the process; however, the most powerful connection would come as a result of a broader understanding of the team he led.

Early in our coaching Randy was having some problems with several of his direct reports. He had weekly staff meetings and several of his team would become discouraged and not participate in full because they thought his approach dictatorial. He would always command the front chair at the end of the table and dictate the meeting taking very little input – again frustrating several members of the team.

Now, he knew he was having problems with the folks and we started discussing why that may be happening. At that point, we started profiling the behavioral style of his team. Once we did this he realized that his team was quite diverse, in fact, most were unlike him, a High D. In fact, his biggest issues were with the High I and S folks.

192

At that point we devised a plan for him to connect with his staff based on their respective styles. He developed his plan and immediately put it to use at the next staff meeting. The first thing he did to connect was to sit not at the head chair but in the middle, which was huge for him. Being a High D, he liked that control and to relinquish that was painful, but he did it anyway. That first "shot across the bow" to connect went over incredibly well. The folks took note and it opened up a friendly and light-hearted discussion that kicked the meeting off on a positive note.

Secondly, he started the meeting by asking for everyone's opinion on how to improve meetings. It was a huge success. In following meetings, he would delegate tasks to lead discussions in the meetings. The result was much more productive meetings and a more productive team.

You need to realize that at first the feeling of giving up power was huge for Randy as it would be for any High D, but he came to realize that this approach was not giving up any power or control whatsoever. In fact, it was doing quite the opposite; it was empowering him.

Oftentimes, you'll find that the High D styles struggle with connecting because they feel like they are giving up the control, but, in fact, when they lead or manage from a point of control they are not powerful at all.

Randy came to realize this and his development as a leader flourished. He was still the confident, aggressive, ambitious and direct High D style Randy, but he put it all in check and knew when and how to wield it based on the styles of those with whom he was interacting. He became a master at reading and connecting and communicating with people. He became a big fan of the Reach Out Approach.

His ability to connect came from my ability to connect with him. I helped him realize that not all people are alike, that we are, indeed, as different as snowflakes and fingerprints, and that his style may not be resonating with all of those people who he came into contact with at work. That simple "team profile" connected with him and, hence, allowed him to connect with his team

Multi-Level Communication – Areas of Benefit:

- One-on-One Personal Relationships

    □ Parent to family

    □ Relationship to family (i.e. wife to her or her husband's family)

- One-on-One Professional Relationships

    □ Managerial – manager to the team

    □ Leader to the team

    □ Teammate to teammates

    □ Sales rep to customer group

    □ Account manager to client group

    □ Customer service to customer group

DID I SAY SNOWFLAKES AND FINGERPRINTS? NOT ONLY INDIVIDUALS BUT TEAMS

When I conduct my workshops this is where the real fun begins because at every level the communication dynamics change in every situation/ company I encounter. Each individual and group dynamic changes because of the unique make-up of each person and team. This makes my job incredibly enjoyable and challenging as I never encounter the same situation twice.

Now for you, learning this skill will greatly enhance your abilities as an effective communicator as you'll not only be successful on a one-on-one basis but with groups as well. This is where this process gets exciting because it teaches skill sets that can improve your life and the lives of others quite dramatically.

Next, we'll go to Chapter 11 to see real-world examples of how the three levels of communication, as well as other creative ways to communicate, can be leveraged.

Chapter 10 - Reach Out Approach Skill Builder Questions:

1. What level of communication do you encounter the most?

2. What levels of communication do you struggle with the most?

3. If you're in a Level 1 Communication scenario:

   - List the individual you come into contact with the most.

   - List their DISC communication style.

   - List a plan of action for communicating with each of them (at Level 1).

4. If you're in a Level 2 Communication scenario:

   - List the individuals you come into contact with the most.

   - List their DISC communication styles.

   - List a plan of action for communicating with each of them (at Level 2).

5. If you're in a Multi-Level Communication scenario:

    • List the individuals on the team you come into contact with
       the most.

    • List their DISC communication styles.

    • List a plan of action for communicating with each of them
       (at Multi-Level).

Chapter 10 Notes:

MASTERY COMMUNICATION IN ACTION!

A s I've said, the ability to successfully apply the Reach Out Approach will enable you to differentiate yourself as an effective communicator. This valuable skill will in turn provide you with the success, prosperity and mastery you not only desire, but also deserve.

We've reviewed each of the steps individually as well as introduced you to the three levels of communication where this process can indeed differentiate you. So now that we are patiently using each chapter as a building block for your success, let's review real-world examples of effective communication and connection in action. You have already read many good examples of this process in action, but the stories in this chapter reveal how this process works in more complex scenarios as well.

In my work I have been fortunate enough to work with many people in many organizations. As I said in a prior chapter, this makes my job incredibly gratifying because no individual or company is the same — each situation provides a unique and fun challenge.

Secondly, I'm able to empower them to use the Reach Out Approach, which in turn improves their lives and creates the all important ripple effect with those with whom they initiate, develop and leverage relationships.

PRACTICAL, REAL-WORLD AND RELEVANT

So now what I would like to share with you are some Reach Out Approach real-world stories. In these examples you will see a variation of all three levels of communication as discussed in the previous chapter. As with all things, nothing is cut and dry. So the examples in this chapter may include complex blends of all three levels. The key is to be aware of all three separately then be prepared to effectively address the unique situations you will face in your world.

As mentioned in the beginning of Chapter 10, if you can master the Reach Out Approach and mirror some of the communication successes as illustrated in these stories, you will differentiate yourself in your field of endeavor, whatever that might be, personally and professionally.

Delegating Leadership – The Coach

Situation - A few years back I received a phone call from Bob Fraser, a former fraternity brother and teammate of mine from Allegheny College. At the time, he was a football coach at the Division I-AA intercollegiate level. He knew of my work with organizations in helping them with communication skills and asked if there was anything I could do for his team as he felt he was struggling to communicate with several of his players. I informed him that I could indeed help him.

Bob is an excellent coach but can sometimes be a tough bird when he communicates. He is from the old school of coaching which means a lot of tough talk. In fact, that seemed to be the way many coaches approach coaching and is indeed the reputation that coaches have. As I mentioned already my college coach worked that way and turned me and many other teammates off. I never responded well to the coach who yelled and screamed or put you in the doghouse without speaking to you or letting you know why. Being a High S, I respond, and always have, to people who are patient and subscribe to two-way open communication. My fondest memories of my favorite coaches were the ones who knew how to approach me to help me thrive. I performed best for those coaches who opened the lines of communication, not closed them. There were guys who responded to the tough love approach, because of my High S style, I was not one of them.

I met with Bob and walked him through the process of recognizing the four communication styles and the importance of each. We then ran the DISC behavioral survey on him and his group of linebackers. We found the results truly insightful. When we reviewed the results on him and his seven linebackers we found all but one had a different communication style from him. In fact, he had a mix of styles on the team but they were heavily High I, in fact, all but one player was not primary or secondary High I. There were also some bordering high S and C's. So, here you have the coach whose style as a High D, is direct, forceful, challenging and aggressive communicating that way to group of guys who are mostly gregarious, expressive, enthusiastic and friendly, High I. If there were clashes or disconnects with the players it was here – communication.

This information was eye opening to my friend who realized that his approach to several of his players might be wrong and the reason why he was not connecting. He was particularly surprised at having so many High I's. The good news was that he has an open mind and was willing to learn and embrace the findings. The question now was what could we do to help him effectively communicate and connect.

Communication Styles
Coach Bob & Linebackers

	D	I	S	C
Coach Bob	74	38	29	52
LB	47	100	29	46
LB	47	46	58	57
LB	53	54	37	57
LB	47	66	52	37
LB	28	66	74	64
LB	74	56	48	15
LB	42	73	52	46

* Note, the bold, dark shade represents the dominant style, the lighter shade secondary high style

The Dynamic – As you can see in the team graph the communication style of the coach is different than most of his players. If he approaches most of them with his High D style he may not effectively communicate with them. This was a team that was very mixed in their styles of communication. What we needed to do was build an action plan to help him not only connect with each of his players based on their unique styles but also how could he leverage their styles as strengths for the team.

We then analyzed the opportunities to communicate and then built a two-pronged action plan. The first being to build a plan for him to communicate with each of his players, based on their respective styles, and then, based on those styles develop a plan where he could flesh out leadership responsibilities for each of them. You see, each of them had unique attributes to bring to the table. It was up to him to identify them and put them to work. This was a big step for him because being a High D he wanted to control the situation and not delegate. The process of seeing the various dynamics of his team helped him realize it was best to delegate and let them take responsibility for leadership. This was also a great relief to him as he was able to free himself to coach and let them take initiative as leaders. Most embraced it because the leadership responsibilities were tailored to their styles; this made it easier for them as it was a natural fit.

Reach Out Approach Action Plan – Bob now had a game plan for how he could/should communicate with his players. It was simple – just adapt his style for effective communication and connection:

- For the sole High D, he could be direct, forceful.

- For the High I's he would engage in much friendlier, personal terms and a much more "rah-rah" manner. His former way of "placing them in the doghouse" was a miserable failure with the High I style as they didn't respond well to it.

- For the High S, he built one on one personal relationships, he criticized them in private and pushed them slowly with his ideas.

- For the High C he focused on the cerebral aspects of the game, illustrating through game films and statistics on how his recommendations as a coach would help them succeed

This approach worked and it also became more fun for him as well. In addition, one of his most difficult connections, the off the chart High I became much more receptive to him and actually improved so much he made the All-Conference team. My friend the coach was communicating big-time!

For fleshing out leadership responsibilities, he decided to do so by their style. But first he educated them on their styles so they understood why he was doing it and to help them communicate better as a team. Now regarding the leadership responsibilities:

- The High D – Was the guy who would "get in someone's face" and act as a disciplinarian to some extent.

- The High I – These were the motivators, the rah-rah types.

- The High S – These guys would approach their teammates one-on-one to help them with their play or technique. They would nurture the camaraderie.

- The High C – These guys, along with the High S would take initiative to study the game plan, their opponent's tendencies and help translate them to their teammates and, most importantly, get the teammates to watch film.

This fleshing out of leadership responsibilities worked out well. It motivated them by their natural behavior style and allowed each of them to take some part in being a leader of the squad. My friend could sit back, see the big picture and become a more effective coach.

In addition to having an All-Conference player, the team had a winning season, despite being decimated by the graduations of three All-Americans and several key seniors the previous year. The team, and especially the linebacker crew, was very green but they pulled off a stellar season. As for my friend, he made it to the big time as he was offered a coaching job at Division I-A Rutgers where he is an assistant coach and practices the art of the Reach Out Approach – impressive ripple effects for all!

As I mentioned in Chapter 2 regarding Generation Y and how they like being communicated to, it is the same with athletes. In speaking with a friend of mine, Jay Hayes, who is defensive line coach for the Cincinnati Bengals, he said athletes today are much more sensitive than in the past. You really do need to learn how to communicate with them on a one-on-one basis. This comment really validates the approach mentioned earlier by successful coaches, Barry Alvarez and Vince Lombardi.

Another good friend of mine, Mark Marshall uses a similar method when coaching wrestlers. He was an excellent wrestler at Indiana State and knows the value of a coach who can communicate. He told me that he really needs to read the style of the athlete and adapt accordingly. He tells stories where he is very firm and direct in his communication with some athletes, whereas, he is more like a mentor and friend with others. As with Barry Alvarez, my friend Mark leverages the "hot buttons" of his squad.

But the story of my friend Bob is also geared towards anyone leading people whether it be a football coach, a manager, leader or parent. Your ability to know the unique dynamics of your team and to communicate, motivate and connect is of utmost importance.

WORKING HIS CHESSBOARD - THE LEADER

Situation – Dan, a region vice president in a company I've worked with had me conduct a communication skills workshop with his three districts. The purpose of the workshop was to improve his communication with the team and, in turn, his district managers and their respective teams. The company was a consumer products company basically selling the exact same product in each of the three districts. The goal of the workshop was to improve his and the team's communication skills, but the workshop took on a new life soon thereafter.

Dan was very interested in having a better understanding of each district manager and their respective teams. He found that his approach to managing and leading them was stressful. His approach worked to different degrees with each of them, but at different times what worked with one didn't work with the other and vice versa.

In addition, he was confounded by some district team dynamics he was encountering. As a whole, one of his district teams seemed more driven and aggressive while others not so much. Meanwhile, another district embraced analytics and used it to sell more effectively and again others not so much. What made things more confusing is they were dealing internally with the launch of a new technology and some embraced it while others didn't. Some were all right with the change in the technology while some hated it and refused to conform. To make matters worse, the launch was not smooth and had some major hiccups that needed to be resolved before being totally accurate and useable; some systems worked, while some didn't.

Now, Dan was used to different styles of people. He realized people were different, but he noted some strong tendencies on two of the teams. They seemed diametrically opposite in all aspects and didn't seem to move together in their approaches, whether it be sales, change or the new technology. He was perplexed but also interested in finding out why. Meanwhile, the third district seemed opposite of the other two in their communication and approach to the business.

As with all communication skills workshops, I ran the DISC behavioral assessment on Dan and all of the people in the three districts. The results we found were very enlightening and really solidified the point that no two individuals and teams are exactly alike.

Dynamic – What became interesting was the communication dynamics of the three districts teams. Of the three teams, none were even close in their respective communication style dynamics. Not one team was alike. One team could be broadly described as aggressive, gregarious and highly outgoing while another team less so and, in fact, more careful, analytic and reserved. Meanwhile, the third team seemed to be a blend of the other two. To understand why, let's look at the three districts separately to learn about their unique communication dynamics.

District #1, led by Juliana was very much a High D and I team. The entire team exhibited either primary or secondary High D or I Behavior (as designated in the graph). They were an outgoing, gregarious and direct team who mirrored their leader Juliana, a strong Primary High D with a fairly secondary High I. Her team was filled with "go getters" who were high risk takers and fearless of change. In addition, they weren't afraid to "mix it up" when conflict was in the air. They were vocal, but never to the point of being negative or disruptive. As Dan said, with this team there was never a dull moment. Juliana and most her team were not afraid to speak their minds.

As the leader of the Region, Dan differed from most of Juliana's team, including Juliana. He was a primary High C but had some secondary High I. Dan realized this as he sometimes clashed with her. He admired her aggressive attitude and that of her team, but sometimes he had to slow her down a bit and become more analytically astute. The findings from the DISC behavioral survey really opened their eyes as it cleared the air and helped them realize why they, at times, disconnected.

Communication Styles
District #1 – Team Juliana

	D	I	S	C
RVP - Dan	35	74	16	75
DM - Juliana	92	86	7	17
Sales Rep	72	74	25	24
Sales Rep	72	52	44	41
Sales Rep	58	86	56	17
Sales Rep	64	25	82	51
Sales Rep	10	86	82	75
Sales Rep	51	52	34	61

For more about Team Juliana, her team was always very good at taking the initiative. They were very aggressive with their clients and not afraid to take risks and chances, even sometimes at the risk of getting a slap on the wrist from the company and customer. By and large this team got along and communicated well. One person on the team was of the Primary C style but he was also secondary High I as well. Meanwhile another was Primary High S but also High D. This entire team was fairly in synch from a behavioral and communication perspective. Even where they had differences, Juliana was able to leverage their styles to her advantage. As an example, she would use the High C to help the rest of the team with the analysis of data. Overall, Juliana was quite progressive in leading her team, but again most of the team were alike in their styles.

Regarding the change initiative and new technology, they were ready to embrace it. Unfortunately, the company fumbled the launch, which meant a lot of bugs and snags. These foul ups deeply frustrated this team who was ready for action. They were told to be ready to go and they were!

Lastly, this was a very productive team and they were always meeting their goals. Although he was a different in style than Juliana and her team Dan liked them and got on well with them, most likely because of his secondary High I. This composite was very enlightening for him as it helped him better understand Team Juliana which in turn helped him better connect and communicate with them.

District #2, led by Barry was very much the opposite of team Juliana. Although Barry and Juliana were alike in their Primary High D communication style, Barry's team was diametrically opposite of him and Juliana's team. Dan as well, being a High C was not like Barry but much more in line with the team and was, at times, at odds with Barry.

Barry's team was dominated with High S and C reps so his team was much more reserved, introverted and analytical than him. They were also significantly more risk averse than Barry and Juliana's team and didn't like change and avoided conflict. Their approach to change and risk frustrated Barry much more than Dan.

Barry was an aggressive "go getter", a high-risk taker and loved changing environments. He liked his team but would sometimes get frustrated with them, however, not nearly as much as they would get with him. They got along fine but at times Barry's pace far exceeded the teams. He would often drive them hard, and they didn't always appreciate it.

Communication Styles
District #2 – Team Barry

	D	I	S	C
RVP - Dan	35	74	16	75
DM - Barry	100	25	11	51
Sales Rep	35	39	69	68
Sales Rep	28	62	82	51
Sales Rep	35	39	93	51
Sales Rep	7	62	93	90
Sales Rep	35	15	93	84
Sales Rep	79	100	56	7

Barry had one sales rep, a High I and D, who appeared to be an outcast. He could be a rabble-rouser with the team, especially when it came to being aggressive and taking risks. This dynamic frustrated Barry, as it hurt teamwork. He could relate with the rep but wanted to see him be much more of a team player.

Barry's team group strength was taking sales data, analyzing it and building sales stories. They were excellent at category management, data analysis and were seen as experts by their customers – a good reason they often made their quota.

Regarding the new technology and change initiative, they were not thrilled at first, but totally fine when the launch was briefly postponed to work out the kinks. They would rather it not be launched than go out with errors and problems.

Lastly, District #3, led by Jorge was yet another interesting team dynamic. His team was a blended mix of all four of the communication styles. In addition, he and Dan were much closer related by style, both High C's, than Juliana and Barry in communication style. Dan felt he not only had more in common, but could communicate better with Jorge. In addition, he felt he had to spend less managerial time with Jorge and his team. Jorge's team had a more diverse team to work with than Juliana and Barry's. His team consisted of High D, I, S and C styles almost equally. Jorge knew this to some extent prior to the workshop but didn't use the broad team dynamics to his advantage by fleshing out responsibilities based on the strengths and weaknesses of each team member. He didn't always communicate as well as he could with several of them. Like Dan, he felt some of the High D and I styles moved too quickly and were a bit too "forward and outgoing" for him. He and Juliana got along well, but he avoided interacting with her "feisty" teammates at meetings. This bothered some on Juliana's team who viewed it negatively.

Communication Styles
District #3 – Team Jorge

	D	I	S	C
RVP - Dan	35	74	16	75
DM - Jorge	8	39	69	98
Sales Rep	28	62	93	51
Sales Rep	72	30	69	33
Sales Rep	72	30	25	61
Sales Rep	58	62	34	41
Sales Rep	28	15	69	95
Sales Rep	43	74	44	68

Although Jorge's team communicated well there were times certain factions would not agree on things. Some folks, High D and I tended to dominate discussions in meetings. The approaches to dealing with the customer and leveraging data varied as well where the High C and S's were in "their zone." Again, Jorge didn't always leverage the individuals to move forward as a cohesive team.

Jorge's team often struggled to make their sales numbers. He felt if he could get his team to share ideas as a group and help one another in solving their customer's problems, they would be more successful as a team.

Regarding the new technology and the change initiative, the obvious styles embraced it while others did not. In other words, the DISC behavior styles "played out" to the tee.

Reach Out Approach Action Plan – As a leader Dan, needed to learn to lead, communicate and connect with the districts differently based on their respective communication styles and team dynamics. Although there were not huge communication and connection issues, there were still gaps and, oftentimes, these gaps posed serious problems. So to help him become a more effective leader, we worked on a four-step process:

1. Empower Dan on how to better initiate, develop and leverage communication with his team by style starting first with his direct reports, the district managers – a Level 1 Communication approach. He developed a plan of action to connect based on each of his district managers' respective styles. His approach to Barry and Juliana were similar as their styles were alike, High D. Meanwhile, he would approach Jorge in another manner, a High C, which wasn't too hard because he was just like him.

2. Empower Dan to understand each respective district's team dynamic based on communication styles. Now that he understood the communication dynamics of each team he not only understood why they did what they did, but knew how to manage expectations with them as well as communicate and connect. If there was another change initiative he knew that Barry's team would not move as quickly as Juliana's or Jorge's, for that matter. He knew what teams would be more aggressive and which ones would not. By understanding this fact, he was able to better manage his expectations with his manager John, a High I, as well. They had a good relationship, but he was much more aware of how John communicated and why he did what he did. It enabled Dan to effectively communicate with John much better than before.

By understanding the communication styles of everyone in his region, he was able to become a much more effective leader and manage situations more effectively. In fact, he started calling the DISC communication charts his "team chessboard." He now knew how to move the pieces for optimal productivity.

3. Empower the district managers to become better at managing upward to Dan. This workshop was not one-sided. It was not solely about how Dan should connect with his team. Yes, that was a part of it, but the other half was how they could connect with him. This was about opening lines of communication with a two-way dialogue – closing the communication gap.

4. Empower the district managers on connecting with their teams and teams with their managers – again the two-way dialogue. In this section we had each team break out and share key dynamics to help them learn to communicate and connect more effectively. In an exercise we had, each team member in their respective district shared the following bits of information with each other. This information was gleaned from the personalized DISC Success Insights® Reports they received:

•   What their value to the team was

•   How people should and should not communicate with them

•   Keys to motivating them

•   Keys to managing them

•   Areas of improvement

Each district manager captured the results from each of their team members then gave them to me. Then, I posted their comments on a one-page document and re-distributed out to the entire region so each team had their communication roadmap, or plan of action, to communicate more effectively. The lines of communication were shared and in the open so all three teams had a plan of action to communicate with one another. The district managers had the roadmap for their teams and most importantly Dan had the communication roadmap for his entire region, which he shared with his managers.

Dan's teams continue to have success. He says each district is working better together and sharing amongst each other. Within each region, the district managers view their team's dynamics as a communication chessboard, to not only know how to communicate and connect, but also to flesh out responsibilities based on style. Each style within each district has a role to play on their team and the region.

Juliana's team is still feisty but considerably more self-aware about connecting with other internal and external customers. Barry is much more conscientious of how he is connecting with his High S and C team. And they, in turn, are much more understanding of Barry's High D style. Jorge has used his chessboard to the fullest as he has a plan of action, not only how to communicate with his team, but how to flesh out responsibilities based on their styles and leveraging their strengths.

Lastly, the Reach Out Approach process we used had a ripple effect on their clients – the numbers keep rolling in and the business keeps growing!

WHY THE BOAT WASN'T TURNING FAST – CHANGE INITIATIVE

Situation – An organization was conducting a major change initiative, conceived by their CEO, which was going slowly. There was really a focus on a new "go to market" strategy in the industry that required a new way of thinking internally. It was of the utmost importance because if they didn't change the strategy, their competition might eat their lunch.

Based on an old culture, the company tended to work in silos and had little interdepartmental communication. The new initiative required them to move out of the silos and become better at sharing and communicating amongst the various departments. This meant departments that normally didn't interface with one another now would need to. In addition, some departments, which were naturally competitive and didn't share, would now have to do so. Again, the key objective was to open lines of communication and get out of silos to create a sharing environment and embrace this new "go to market" strategy.

Overall, the initiative was going slow. Primarily because, most of the departments were not willing to get out of their silos and cooperate with other departments. In fact, many were fighting this initiative tooth and nail.

The company brought me in to assess the change initiative team and gain an understanding of why the initiative was moving slowly and also how I could help the team communicate better. I had been working with several managers in the organization and knew of the change initiative. I was asked to use the DISC behavioral survey to assess the team and then conduct a workshop to help them communicate and connect better and help them move the change initiative in the right direction.

Dynamic – Upon running the survey I quickly found out a big reason why the change initiative was moving so slowly. As I ran the communication survey on the group, I found that they were heavily C and S oriented, highly risk averse and very concerned about the effects of change.

Communication Styles
Change Management Initiative Team

	D	I	S	C
Team Leader	72	10	34	90
Team Member	8	62	69	90
Team Member	7	39	93	98
Team Member	8	25	93	100
Team Member	92	100	11	7
Team Member	7	62	100	90
Team Member	51	62	34	61
Team Member	72	9	44	90
Team Member	43	10	69	90
Team Member	10	52	69	90
Team Member	17	74	56	68
Team Member	58	8	82	84
Team Member	43	62	69	33
Team Member	28	52	69	61

When reviewing the communication dynamics of the team as you can see it was heavily C and S dominated. This is not a group, based on their scores, that changes quickly. Regarding change, High S style needs time to prepare, while the High C is concerned about the effects of it. Regarding risk, the High S is a moderately low risk taker, while the High C is very low.

This was an eye opening finding. It begged the question, how can a team of such risk averse, non-change agent folks be leading the change initiative? It was no wonder that the initiative was moving so slowly.

There were other styles on the team, but again it was very heavily weighted to the High S and C. Again, as I said earlier in this book, there is no right or wrong communication style. However, when you are conducting a change initiative and it's not going well, the fact that it is a High S and C team is very instructive.

Regarding the team dynamics, they were not communicating well amongst each other as well as with the folks they needed to interact within the organization whose help they needed to get the initiative going. Most importantly, the members of the team didn't feel comfortable with the changes which in turn affected their enthusiasm and, hence, the over all success. They were not aggressive and were having many issues getting the department heads to move forward. In addition, some of the department heads were High C styles as well, so they naturally weren't embracing the new philosophy.

This posed a serious issue as the company made a huge investment in this new "go to market" strategy. Keep in mind, this new strategy was imperative for future growth and in securing an advantage and differentiating point against their competition. In other words, a lot was riding on it.

Reach Out Approach Action Plan – There were several options in addressing the situation. We could have created a new team with a more diverse set of behavioral styles in the mix, but the company felt they had too much already invested in the process to "blow this team up" and start all over.

The next option was to work with this team to help them understand their willingness for dealing with change. Another organization was going to come in and help them then identify what they needed to do to "kick start" the program. I was to simply help the team connect with each other and other colleagues they would be interfacing with in this process. In other words, I was working with them to "open up their eyes" to see why they may be not embracing the initiative. Then based on team dynamics help them to initiate, develop and leverage with each other as a team – and with those all-important department heads whose input was imperative to the success of the initiative and company.

So, basically, we ran the surveys and shared the results with them. They were quite interested in the findings and realized that they were, indeed, not embracing the new initiative. What seemed to resonate with them the most was their communication styles and how they connected or disconnected with the department heads. We did some work in profiling the various department heads to identify their styles and then developed a plan of action to connect with each of them. Out of the top department heads, a majority of those were High S and C as well. So it was no surprise that they weren't embracing the initiative.

First, we developed a "communication roadmap" similar to the one I discussed in the previous story about the VP named Dan. This opened up communication amongst the change initiative team – they connected.

Then, we built a dialogue and approach to use for each of the department heads based on their style. We practiced this new approach. The point of the exercise was to help each person develop an action plan to connect with each of the other department heads based on style. This allowed each member of the change initiative team to apply the Reach Out Approach with the folks responsible for making this plan work.

Previously, there was not one lick of initiating, developing and leveraging. So now my job was to pass the change initiative back to the other consulting group for the re-launch. The group was much more motivated and in synch. We connected, now it was their turn to make the big connection – successfully implementing the new "go to market" strategy.

IT'S NO BARKING MATTER –
COMMUNICATING WITH THE CONSUMER

Situation – One of the most enjoyable clients I have is in the pet foods industry. This company has thoroughly embraced reaching out, connecting and communicating at all levels in the organization – the leaders, managers and sales rep level.

The only group at this point that I did not work with was their demo managers. These were the folks who managed retail demonstrators, the people who greet consumers in stores, give them samples and then provide them with sales material relevant to their pets needs. This company has superior demo teams but they brought me in to work with the managers on their communication skills – helping them connect with their teams.

The workshops could not have gone better. The folks were terrific and really embraced the learning. There was, however, a question that all of them had for me. "How can our demonstrators use this tool to connect at retail with the consumer? In other words, how can we educate them on this wonderful behavioral tool to help them connect at retail with the consumers, a Level 2 Communication?" Now the problem was that they did not have a budget to bring me in to train all of the retail demonstrators. But the demo managers had meetings to train their teams. The question was how do they translate the DISC behavioral communication fundamentals to a part-time retail demonstrator. We didn't need the retail demonstrators to be experts on DISC communication, but wanted to pass some "turn-key" skill sets to them, so they could better connect with the consumer. What could we do? Brainstorm!

Dynamic: At that point, I let them break out into groups and brainstorm some ideas. Then magic happened in one of the groups. They said they knew they needed an easy way to help the retail demonstrators learn and remember the four styles, in addition an easy way to leverage it with the consumer. One of the group leaders said, "We sell dog food, why don't we translate the four DISC behavior styles into dogs that relate to the style?" In other words, to help the retail demonstrators understand DISC as Dominance, Influence, Steadiness and Compliance we would just substitute dog types in place of the DISC name.

So a High D became a Doberman, a High I became a Jack Russell, a High S became a Labrador and a High C became a Chihuahua. This way the demonstrators could relate the styles to the dog – instant connection!

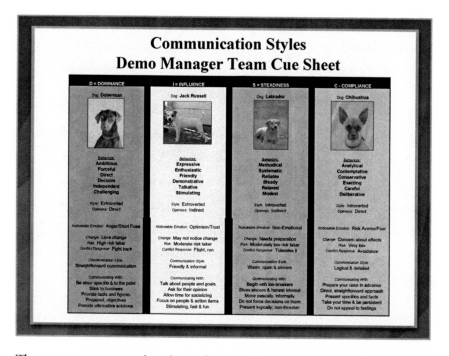

The next step was to then have the retail demo managers relate the dog style to the consumer. So if a very bubbly, happy, gregarious consumer came into the store they would be a Jack Russell style (High I). If a reserved, friendly quiet consumer came in they would be a Lab (High S). Then lastly, based on the dog style, the retail demo rep would know how to dialogue and communicate with the customer as well as what type of collateral to give them that is relevant to their pet's need.

As an example, with the High D or C customers, the retail demo rep would share fact based information and company collateral on how their dog food benefits the dog – things like shiny coat, less shedding, easy on stomach, etc. If a High I or S style came in they would share a testimonial of how the product worked with their pet or someone they knew. They would also show a photo of a dog, preferably theirs, to illustrate the benefits of their pet food (again showing a photo of a shiny coat, less shedding, etc.).

The key to this approach was to help the retail demo rep to connect with the customer to convert them to their product in addition to possibly buying more products in the store (like pet snacks and toys).

This was vital as it provided a value added benefit for the stores and they loved it. The retail demo managers thus connected with the stores because the stores increased their overall sales as well – it was a "win-win-win" – for the company, store and consumer. Not to mention, it added a lot of fun at retail. And let's not forget the dogs who had shinier coats, happier stomachs and less shedding – talk about a ripple effect. I'll bet you didn't know it would reach animals as well. I even think my F&M buyer Joel would have liked it, too.

LEARNING TO DANCE – ACCOUNT PENETRATION

Another area where Reach Out Approach can pay off is areas where there is a gatekeeper in the way of a key decision maker – account penetration. This is symbolic of any industry. Take pharmaceuticals as an example, a sales rep must get through a gatekeeper to get to a key decision maker or a Level 2 Communication approach. In pharmaceuticals, it would be working through the nurse or office manager to get to the physician. Essentially, account penetration is all about getting to key decision makers.

There are many industries or situations when a gatekeeper is used to block access to a key decision maker. Not only must you connect with the key decision maker, you need to connect to the gatekeepers first. This Reach Out Approach process will enable you to become effective in this scenario as well. I've been hired to work with several companies where this dynamic is present.

Situation – The basic process is that I run the DISC behavioral survey on the sales reps or account managers so they know their communication styles – enabling them to reach out. Then I taught them to profile the DISC communication style, not only the key decision maker's style but that of the gatekeepers as well. The point was if they could connect and penetrate the gatekeeper they could see the key decision maker sooner. By understanding the gatekeepers' DISC behavior style the sales rep/account manager could, in turn, connect. The sales rep/account manager could build rapport quicker and, in turn, see the key decision maker sooner.

Then, by profiling the key decision maker, they hopefully could connect, communicate and accomplish whatever it was they needed to accomplish – i.e. sales.

Dynamic – In addition to the profiling, I work with my clients to develop communication dialogue and a process for delivering certain collateral to the key decision maker based on style – similar to what we do with my pet food client. If the key decision maker were a High D or C, the sales rep/account manager would use certain communication that would appeal to the respective style. They also deliver collateral that would appeal to that style. In this instance, it would be analytic data, research, testing type data, basically, any fact-based information. If the key decision maker was a High I or S they would give similar collateral, but also include information that focuses on benefits to people via real life testimonials.

The point of the Reach Out Approach is to gain the desired results.

THREE BASE FUNDAMENTALS
TO ENSURE SUCCESS

The point behind these stories is to illustrate the various creative ways companies use the DISC behavioral assessment as a way to use the Reach Out Approach. Whether it was as a coach and/or manager to their teams or sales reps to their clients, the point was to:

- Initiate – Make the effort to understand the human dynamic

- Develop – Make the effort to create the connection between their styles and the styles of others

- Leverage – Adapt for effective communication

And in turn, create a ripple effect touching many others.

In addition, I wanted to illustrate the importance of mastering the art of effective communication. These stories really validate how successful work-related results are in direct correlation with effective communication. Whether the example was of a coach, a leader, a team member or a specific situation (the change initiative), the ability to understand the communication and behavioral dynamics was of the utmost importance to the successful results that were gleaned. This again proves the point that the ability to have true success is with and through people. Your ability to maneuver through the many people dynamics you will face will indeed determine your success or failure of any endeavor.

These stories also illustrate that success is often gained indirectly through people. It may not be your initial contact. Oftentimes, you must get things done by having someone else do it, just like Dan in the example previously mentioned in this chapter. He most often needed to work through his direct reports, Juliana, Barry and Jorge to get things done. He worked through them to better motivate and communicate with their respective teams.

Lastly, this chapter also illustrates that effective communication is an art. It can be learned, but it must be worked at in order to become a master. The three steps of initiating, developing and leveraging is the foundation. Learn to master these three steps and they will provide you with the solid foundation you need for success.

Reach Out Helpful Tool

Learn more about your communication style

Would you like to view a sample of the Success Insights Report® mentioned in this chapter?

The Success Insights Report® is a tailored and personalized report that will identify your communication style and empower you to become a master communicator.

If interested, then visit the website below:

www.reachoutapproach.com/development

Chapter 11 - Reach Out Approach Skill Builder Questions:

1. Do any of the scenario's in this chapter resonate with you? If so, which one and why?

2. Upon reviewing your personal scenario's, what are ways you can think out of the box in communicating with others, individually and/or team-based?

3. Based on your communication style, what is holding you back in effectively communicating with others?

4. Develop a communication chess board. Use the process of reading styles you learned in Chapter 8 along with developing your communication plan of action you learned in Chapter 9 to develop your chessboard:

    • If you are an individual, then create one for up to five people you interact with.

    • If you are a manager or leader, create one for your team.

    • If you are on a team, create one for your teammates.

- If you are in sales or account management, create one for your customers.

Chapter 11 Notes:

THE REACH OUT APPROACH: THE BIG PICTURE

The one person who has influenced my life the most by reaching out, communicating and connecting with me is my mentor Santo Laqautra. I have never met anyone better at communicating and connecting than him. The key component behind it is his genuine caring for others and to help others.

When I think of my friend and mentor, I can't help but think of this insightful quote by actor Sidney Poitier as it epitomized Santo's approach of effective communication:

"Living consciously involves being genuine; it involves listening and responding to others honestly and openly; it involves being in the moment."

Whenever I'm interacting with him he is definitely "in the moment!" It seems like nothing else in the world matters – he is totally engaged, listening and responding – and most importantly he is always genuine.

I was fortunate enough to have met Santo twenty-eight years ago when I was a senior in college, interviewing for my first job. On this particular day, I had an interview scheduled with a company named

Beecham Products, a manufacturer of various consumer products, namely Aqua-Fresh Toothpaste. At the time, Santo was Director of Training and Manpower Deployment. I actually didn't have any intentions of working for Beecham, but a friend got me the interview and I just happened to be in Pittsburgh for another reason so I went to the interview. I was actually in town to attend my final interview at Northwestern Mutual Life. I already had three interviews with them and was totally impressed and excited. I liked everyone I met there, especially the senior leadership that were quite impressive. I had friends who worked there. I would be working in the impressive US Steel Building in Pittsburgh and most importantly they were recruiting me, which was impressive for a twenty-two-year-old kid just about to land his first job out of college.

So there I was, walking into the Beecham Products headquarters to interview for a sales job with a guy who had a crazy Italian name, Santo Laquatra. Throughout the morning all I could think about that day was working for Northwestern Mutual in the sixty-four-floor US Steel Building, the tallest building in Pittsburgh. I couldn't wait to get through the morning interview with Beecham so I could go to the final interview at Northwestern Mutual Life where they were going to make me a job offer later that afternoon. It just couldn't happen soon enough, if I could only get through the interview with this guy named Santo.

Then something amazing happened – I met Santo. In my entire life I cannot remember being so taken by someone, he was so impressive. He was a great listener, he was engaging, caring, interesting, tough yet fair – and most importantly, genuine. I never had such an interview or met such a wonderful, intriguing person. He asked great questions and really listened and I knew it because his follow up questions proved it.

He was genuine. He reached out, connected and communicated with me.

After the interview, I went to the Northwestern Mutual interview and everything had changed. All I could do was think about my interview with Santo and how impressed I was with him. As the GM and VP of sales at Northwestern were raving about me and ultimately offering me a job, the only thing I could think about was "schlepping" Aqua-Fresh toothpaste for a guy named Santo at a company called Beecham Products. Santo's connection was that strong. In fact, I put the Northwestern offer on hold as I continued to interview with Beecham. I went through three more interviews, spent a day "in the field" with a sales representative and eventually Beecham offered me a job. I said yes to them and no to Northwestern.

I never worked for Santo directly but attended many of his workshops and spent many days working in the field with him. But he always said he had an open-door policy and to call him at anytime. He had quite an incredible reputation in the company and was truly loved by everyone. In fact, he has remained an influence in my life until this very day as both my friend and mentor. He is a consultant like me; you might say that I have followed in his footsteps.

Santo not only reached out and connected in that first interview, he has done it many times. In fact, he helped catapult my career at a time when it was snowballing downhill.

When Beecham hired me they brought me in as an entry-level sales representative in the Pittsburgh suburbs. My first manager placed the district supervisor in charge of my training. Unfortunately, the district supervisor was not a good manager or trainer. In fact, he was a pretty bad.

After six months, I was far behind in my development as a sales rep. I was not performing well and I knew it. I was well behind my colleagues in every sales attribute we were measured on. I was struggling with my customers and couldn't seem to "get it." This continued for another six months – a whole year and not much to show for it. It got worse, my sales and performance numbers were poor, I had no confidence and started calling headhunters looking for another job. It was a bad feeling knowing I was failing at my first job out of college. It got so bad that I even feared getting fired.

It was at that time I thought of reaching out to Santo, after all he said he had an open-door policy and that I should never hesitate to give him a call. Again, he was not my manager, but we did form enough of a relationship where I felt I could reach out to him for help. I called him and we met for breakfast.

When I discussed my situation he let me know he had not heard any-thing negative about my performance, but that he understood my situation. I told him that I wanted to leave the company and asked if he could help me. He said he understood totally and that he would help in any way he could; I felt so relieved. I was sad and a bit ashamed that I did not succeed at my first job. In fact, I felt a bit like a quitter and even let Santo down, but I just felt I was too far behind in my develop-ment and that maybe this job was not for me. I was relieved that Santo would help me exit gracefully.

Well, that sly dog, had another idea in mind. Unbeknownst to me, Santo approached my manager and read him the riot act. He knew the district manager in charge of my training was bad, so he told my boss to get Steve, another training manager, and get him up to speed ASAP! He reminded the others that they had all had a hand in interviewing and hiring me and that they knew I had skills. He made it clear that they had failed me.

It was a time in the corporate environment when managers took responsibility and were accountable for good hiring practices and successfully training and developing people. My boss got the message and placed another new manager on the case who became responsible for training me. This new manager was an "up and comer" in the company and had an awesome reputation for training and developing talent. He was also an intimidating guy. His name was Tim. Tim took over my training and development and an interesting thing happened – I flourished! Tim was so good at training on the fundamentals that I had solid ground to stand on. He taught me fundamentals that were so important to the job. From that point on my career blossomed. I ended up spending a wonderful ten years with the company and a total of nineteen years in the consumer packaged goods industry. I worked many roles and had various responsibilities. All of this because my skills were built by a great trainer who knew how to reach out, connect and communicate, and most importantly because a wonderful man named Santo reached out, connected and communicated as well.

This story resonates with me for several reasons; my career could have taken a bad turn south and who knows where that would have led? The ripple effect could have taken a severe turn towards the negative rather than the positive. When I was struggling and had low confidence... who knows what would have happened if I had quit, it could have snowballed. It is never good to quit something when one's confidence is low. In fact, I have seen this phenomenon happen to many folks in the workplace. This is why I am so passionate about training and developing people. Training and development are the keys to everybody's success in the workplace or any field of endeavor we choose.

Fortunately because of Santo and Tim, I gained a valuable skill set, confidence and a successful nineteen-year career was initiated. The situation ended on a happy note rather than a sad one. The point being, when people reach out the positive repercussions are endless. *The ripple effect is forever!*

The reason I share this story is that it illustrates what the Reach Out Approach is all about as well as the powerful ripple effect that takes place. This was illustrated many times throughout this book, but the story of Santo Laquatra is the one that by far has most influenced my life and has driven my passion for effective communication. Because of my relationship with Santo, I know what the Reach Out Approach can do for people's lives. It is why I am passionate about it, why I speak about it, why I train on it and why I have dedicated my life around it. It is my passion!

THE DOLLARS AND SENSE OF THE REACH OUT APPROACH!

There is another fantastic upside to the Reach Out Approach: It makes sense from a monetary perspective. Doesn't it make sense that happy, productive employees affect the top-line in the positive? Think about it from these two points:

- Happy, productive employees affect top-line because they are performing better; they are more productive and business prospers.

- Happy, productive employees affect the bottom line because they are staying in your company and not leaving; in other words, turn rates are much lower, which saves money.

In the book, *Topgrading*, author Bradford Smart states that miss-hires alone can cost a company up to 15 times base salary[38]. That is just a miss-hire, so also consider how much non-productive, unhappy employees can cost a company. Employees you've invested in who become disenchanted but stay with the company as unmotivated employees, is a loss of money as well. Now, to be sure, some losses are OK, especially if someone is just "not the right fit" for a job. But, in most cases, I've seen the issues revolve more around bad hiring and training practices and most noticeably, poor communication. Unfortunately, most companies don't realize the ill affects miss-hires and unhappy employees have on the bottom line. As Bradford Smart notes, it is significant.

THE REACH OUT APPROACH IN THE WORKPLACE

One of the most important ways companies can maximize performance of employees is to invest fully in training and coaching. Two surveys validate this importance from the productivity perspective:

- An article in *Public Personnel Management* revealed the following in a recent study:

  □ Training increases productivity by over 22%

  □ Training along with coaching increased productivity by over 88%

This last fact, the 88% increase in productivity becomes even more important when we tie it to how Generation Y wants to connect in the workplace – we discussed this in Chapter 2.

- A study in Manchester Review revealed that companies that invested in executive coaching received a return of investment of more than five times the cost of coaching

So there you have it, reaching out and connecting is not only the right thing to do, but it also benefits you on a dollars and "sense" basis as well.

So with that said, the people-centric Reach Out Approach can make for happy employees who, in turn, lift the top-line.

THE REACH OUT APPROACH
ON THE PERSONAL SIDE

Just think of all the peace and happiness – and less agitation – you will have in your personal life by becoming a master communicator. Think of parents effectively communicating with their children, spouses communicating with one another and family members communicating with each other. Your relationships with your mates, family members and community will be that much more rewarding because you'll be a master at effective communication.

THIS, LADIES AND GENTLEMEN, IS A HUMAN BEING!

As I close this book, I hope you clearly understand my comment, "This, ladies and gentlemen, is a human being." I tell folks often, our creator did not place computers, iPods, Blackberries and fax machines on this earth, but people; human beings were put on this earth. Let's not forget that fact.

Yes, tools and technological gadgets help us communicate but they should not be a substitute for human interaction, especially when the situation involves something important and includes the goal of touching the lives of others.

We can make our lives and the lives of those we interact with much better when we apply the Reach Out Approach. As I said, and as you've seen in the examples I provided, you can create a positive ripple effect that can touch so many others. So take the initiative to do so and in turn achieve the success, prosperity and mastery that you and so many others desire *and deserve!*

Don't wait for others. Be the spark that ignites the flame – master the art of effective communication with the Reach Out Approach today!

Reach Out FROM Steve

Reach Out Approach mastery - **The art of effective communication**

Want to take the Reach Out Approach to the next level?

Do you want specific action plans for your next steps?

Take 2-3 minutes to watch author Steve Gavatorta in action as he shares a few more nuggets you can use to get even more results.

www.reachoutapproach.com/nextsteps

And don't forget to keep Reaching Out to Steve and others as well.

www.reachoutapproach.com/communicate

Chapter 12 - Reach Out Approach Skill Builder Questions:

1. What are the three biggest nuggets of wisdom you learned from reading this book and how will you apply them in your life?

2. List all of the people you will begin using the Reach Out Approach with today?

3. What action plans will you immediately develop to use the Reach Out Approach with them?

4. Have you met the five goals you set for yourself in Chapter 1? If not, what will you do to achieve them?

Chapter 12 Notes:

For more information about Steve Gavatorta Group, Inc. please feel free to visit the following websites:

- The Company - www.gavatorta.com

- Steve Gavatorta – www.gavatorta.com/stevegavatorta.htm

- Steve Gavatorta Group Blog - www.gavatorta.com/blog/

- Motivational Quotes - www.gavatorta.com/quote.htm

- Motivational Cards – www.gavatorta.com/cards.htm

For more information about The Reach Out Approach, please feel free to visit the following websites:

- Reach Out Approach Home Page – www.reachoutapproach.com

- Products – www.reachoutapproach.com/products

- Coaching/Training/Webinars – www.reachoutapproach.com

- Reach Out Approach Newsletter - www.gavatorta.com/newsletter.htm

REFERENCES CITED

CHAPTER 2

1) Novations (2007 September) Why does senior management have a hard time connecting with employees? *T+D Magazine*, 17

2) Bingham, T. & Galagan, P (2008 June) Doing good while doing well. *T+D Magazine*, 33 & 34

3) Novations (2008 June) Does senior management encounter problems communicating with any of the following employees? *T+D Magazine*, 21

4) Hefter, R. Connecting with Generation Y, Novations.com, URL http://www.novations.com/search.html?query=rebecca+heftner&x=20&y=10

5) Coleman, H The millennials and the arrival of the next generation. Industrial Distribution, 1/10/2008 8:50 AM, URL http://www.inddist.com/article/CA6519451.html

CHAPTER 4

6) Bonnstetter, Bill J., and Judy I. Suiter. (2007). *The universal language DISC: A reference manual.* (Vol. 11, pp. 44-45). Arizona. Target Training International, Ltd.

7) Bonnstetter, Bill J., and Judy I. Suiter. (2007). *The universal language DISC: A reference manual.* (Vol. 11, pp. 48-50). Arizona. Target Training International, Ltd.

8) Bonnstetter, Bill J., and Judy I. Suiter. (2007). *The universal language DISC: A reference manual.* (Vol. 11, pp. 51). Arizona. Target Training International, Ltd.

9) Bonnstetter, Bill J., and Judy I. Suiter. (2007). *The universal language DISC: A reference manual.* (Vol. 11, pp. 54). Arizona. Target Training International, Ltd.

CHAPTER 5

10) Bonnstetter, Bill J., and Judy I. Suiter. (2007). *The universal language DISC: A reference manual.* (Vol. 11, pp. 59-60). Arizona. Target Training International, Ltd.

11) Bonnstetter, Bill J., and Judy I. Suiter. (2007). *The universal language DISC: A reference manual.* (Vol. 11, pp. 63-64). Arizona. Target Training International, Ltd.

12) Bonnstetter, Bill J., and Judy I. Suiter. (2007). *The universal language DISC: A reference manual.* (Vol. 11, pp. 65). Arizona. Target Training International, Ltd.

13) Bonnstetter, Bill J., and Judy I. Suiter. (2007). *The universal language DISC: A reference manual.* (Vol. 11, pp. 68). Arizona. Target Training International, Ltd.

CHAPTER 6

14) Bonnstetter, Bill J., and Judy I. Suiter. (2007). *The universal language DISC: A reference manual.* (Vol. 11, pp. 73-74). Arizona. Target Training International, Ltd.

15) Bonnstetter, Bill J., and Judy I. Suiter. (2007). *The universal language DISC: A reference manual.* (Vol. 11, pp. 77-79). Arizona. Target Training International, Ltd.

16) Bonnstetter, Bill J., and Judy I. Suiter. (2007). *The universal language DISC: A reference manual.* (Vol. 11, pp. 80). Arizona. Target Training International, Ltd.

17) Bonnstetter, Bill J., and Judy I. Suiter. (2007). *The universal language DISC: A reference manual.* (Vol. 11, pp. 83). Arizona. Target Training International, Ltd.

CHAPTER 7

18) Bonnstetter, Bill J., and Judy I. Suiter. (2007). *The universal language DISC: A reference manual.* (Vol. 11, pp. 88-89). Arizona. Target Training International, Ltd.

19) Bonnstetter, Bill J., and Judy I. Suiter. (2007). *The universal language DISC: A reference manual.* (Vol. 11, pp. 92-93). Arizona. Target Training International, Ltd.

20) Bonnstetter, Bill J., and Judy I. Suiter. (2007). *The universal language DISC: A reference manual.* (Vol. 11, pp. 94). Arizona. Target Training International, Ltd.

21) Bonnstetter, Bill J., and Judy I. Suiter. (2007). *The universal language DISC: A reference manual.* (Vol. 11, pp. 97). Arizona. Target Training International, Ltd.

CHAPTER 9

22) Bonnstetter, Bill J., and Judy I. Suiter. (2007). *The universal language DISC: A reference manual.* (Vol. 11, pp. 51). Arizona. Target Training International, Ltd.

23) Bonnstetter, Bill J., and Judy I. Suiter. (2007). *The universal language DISC: A reference manual.* (Vol. 11, pp. 51). Arizona. Target Training International, Ltd.

24) Bonnstetter, Bill J., and Judy I. Suiter. (2007). *The universal language DISC: A reference manual.* (Vol. 11, pp. 52). Arizona. Target Training International, Ltd.

25) Bonnstetter, Bill J., and Judy I. Suiter. (2007). *The universal language DISC: A reference manual.* (Vol. 11, pp. 53). Arizona. Target Training International, Ltd.

26) Bonnstetter, Bill J., and Judy I. Suiter. (2007). *The universal language DISC: A reference manual.* (Vol. 11, pp. 65). Arizona. Target Training International, Ltd.

27) Bonnstetter, Bill J., and Judy I. Suiter. (2007). *The universal language DISC: A reference manual.* (Vol. 11, pp. 65). Arizona. Target Training International, Ltd.

28) Bonnstetter, Bill J., and Judy I. Suiter. (2007). *The universal language DISC: A reference manual.* (Vol. 11, pp. 66). Arizona. Target Training International, Ltd. 66

29) Bonnstetter, Bill J., and Judy I. Suiter. (2007). *The universal language DISC: A reference manual.* (Vol. 11, pp. 66). Arizona. Target Training International, Ltd.

30) Bonnstetter, Bill J., and Judy I. Suiter. (2007). *The universal language DISC: A reference manual.* (Vol. 11, pp. 80). Arizona. Target Training International, Ltd.

31) Bonnstetter, Bill J., and Judy I. Suiter. (2007). *The universal language DISC: A reference manual.* (Vol. 11, pp. 80). Arizona. Target Training International, Ltd.

32) Bonnstetter, Bill J., and Judy I. Suiter. (2007). *The universal language DISC: A reference manual.* (Vol. 11, pp. 81). Arizona. Target Training International, Ltd.

33) Bonnstetter, Bill J., and Judy I. Suiter. (2007). *The universal language DISC: A reference manual.* (Vol. 11, pp. 81). Arizona. Target Training International, Ltd.

34) Bonnstetter, Bill J., and Judy I. Suiter. (2007). *The universal language DISC: A reference manual.* (Vol. 11, pp. 94). Arizona. Target Training International, Ltd.

35) Bonnstetter, Bill J., and Judy I. Suiter. (2007). *The universal language DISC: A reference manual.* (Vol. 11, pp. 94). Arizona. Target Training International, Ltd.

36) Bonnstetter, Bill J., and Judy I. Suiter. (2007). *The universal language DISC: A reference manual.* (Vol. 11, pp. 95). Arizona. Target Training International, Ltd.

37) Bonnstetter, Bill J., and Judy I. Suiter. (2007). *The universal language DISC: A reference manual.* (Vol. 11, pp. 95). Arizona. Target Training International, Ltd.

CHAPTER 12

38) Smart, B.D, (2005). Topgrading: How to hire, coach and keep A players, 7

TreeNeutral™

Advantage Media Group is proud to be a part of the Tree Neutral™ program. Tree Neutral offsets the number of trees consumed in the production and printing of this book by taking proactive steps such as planting trees in direct proportion to the number of trees used to print books. To learn more about Tree Neutral, please visit **www. treeneutral.com**. To learn more about Advantage Media Group's commitment to being a responsible steward of the environment, please visit **www.advantagefamily.com/green**

The Reach Out Approach is available in bulk quantities at special discounts for corporate, institutional, and educational purposes. To learn more about the special programs Advantage Media Group offers, please visit **www.KaizenUniversity.com** or call 1.866.775.1696.

Advantage Media Group is a leading publisher of business, motivation, and self-help authors. Do you have a manuscript or book idea that you would like to have considered for publication? Please visit **www. amgbook.com**

CPSIA information can be obtained at www.ICGtesting.com
Printed in the USA
240910LV00001B/145/P

9 781599 320984